To: Melissa

Life is about
" you " make it out to
With God's help!

Sincerely, Glen
Williams

Betrayal in The Church

The Bishop and My Wife—A True Story
of Surviving Adultery

by
Glenn A. Williams

Bloomington, IN Milton Keynes, UK

authorHOUSE

AuthorHouse™
1663 Liberty Drive, Suite 200
Bloomington, IN 47403
www.authorhouse.com
Phone: 1-800-839-8640

First published by AuthorHouse 3/17/2009

ISBN: 978-1-4343-0632-6 (sc)

Printed in the United States of America
Bloomington, Indiana

This book is printed on acid-free paper.

I would like to dedicate this book to my family. My children, Faaith, Daavid, and Chaarity, have been such strong troopers in this campaign to complete this project. Also to my wife of 23 years, who the devil swore to separate me from. I love you more now than ever before, because I know me more, and most importantly I know God more. There were many people that helped me, and I promise you I will miss some one if I was to go back 4 years to list everyone. Thanks to everyone that had a part in our healing and our success. God bless, and God respect to you and yours.

The foreword to this book was written by a man of God that I have come to respect and appreciate beyond measure. He is a man of deep passion, and sincere love for God. There are no words to express how much I appreciate him. Thank you so much Apostle Stacy Spencer.

After being in Memphis, Tennessee for 6 months we finally found a church that we were comfortable with. I personally thought that it was too *hip hop*, but the word of God was outstanding. My kids and wife loved it, but because of my strong religious upbringing, I felt that it was way too liberal. This ministry would soon change my life forever. It was so real, sincere, honest and fun. Pastor Stacy, preached with such conviction. I would often see and hear him preach his own real pain, with crocodile tears flowing from his eyes. It changed me. I felt like I didn't have to hide any more, and that I could start to heal. He also challenged my religious/traditional/self-righteous side. I didn't even know that it was there, but it was and it had to be dealt with.

Now I know that I am the righteousness of God through Jesus Christ. No longer do I have to feel bad because of my shortcomings, and no longer do I have to keep coming up short, because of what Jesus did.

Forward by
Stacy L. Spencer

Surviving betrayal in marriage has always been one of the hardest things to deal with much less share with the public. Often times, we think of women who have had to deal with the ripping of the heart by their husbands who have gone off to commit adultery behind their back. In this book we see first hand that men also suffer from the hurt of betrayal. For many generations now, it has almost been accepted that extra-martial relationships are part of the norm of society with TV shows like Desperate Housewives, and the many soap operas filled with betrayal in relationships. What is missing though is the transparency of people who have survived that betrayal and ultimately how to deal with the hurt from a Christian perspective.

Glenn Williams has dealt openly and honestly about his struggle to overcome the hurt of being caught up in a love triangle with his Bishop and his wife. One cannot imagine the double sided hurt of adultery involving one's soul mate and the one who should be looking after your soul. There hasn't been a more honest look into the window of inner church hurt than with this book by Glenn. He takes you from the initial discovery and the unfolding layers of hurt that he has had to pull back in order to recover.

There is an African proverb that says, "You cannot heal that which you try to conceal." So many people walk around trying to hide their scars but like Jesus. Glenn asks you to put your finger in his wounds so you can learn from his pain.

This is a redemptive journey through the life of a husband and a wife who fight the very imps and demons of hell in order to get back a marriage that many would have abandoned. This book is a real look at how Christians survive the worse betrayal one can imagine by living out the principles that many of us only sing and preach about but have never had to put them into practice. Glenn's book shows us that we can do ALL things through Christ who strengthens us. No matter where you are in your marriage or relationship, there is hope for you as you read about this couples journey back from hell and heartbreak. They personify what the Psalmist said in chapter 139:7-8, "Where can I go from your Spirit? Where can I flee from your presence? " If I go up to the heavens, you are there; if in make my bed in the depths, you are there." How many of us through bad decisions in our marriage have made our beds in hell? How many times have we hurt the ones we love the most only to discover our beds are in hell? I'm glad that Glenn Williams takes us on the road to recovery and doesn't leave us there.

It is through forgiveness, prayer, crying, counseling, and soul searching that Glenn leads us back to restoration where all those who have been wounded by adultery can say like the writer of Hebrews, MARRIAGE should be honored by all, and the marriage bed kept pure. After reading this book you will hear Jesus asking the woman who was caught in adultery in John 8, "Woman, where are they? Has no one condemned you?" "no one, sir," she said. "then neither do I condemn you," Jesus declared. "Go now and leave your life of sin."

Stacy L. Spencer
Chief Apostle Officer

Contents

Preface

I'm forty-five years old, and I just recently watched the story of the Williams' family. It featured Venus and Serena Williams--the number one and two players in the World of Women's Tennis. They have completely shattered the record books, much like Tiger Woods and Michael Jordan in their respective sports.

After viewing the DVD on the Williams family, I became a little curious to know if we were related in anyway. Our last names are the same, we both have prematurely gray hair, and we both love tennis. So, I called my Dad. I wasn't entirely sure if his last name was really Williams, and soon my suspicion was confirmed. Not only was I not related to the Williams sisters, but also my last name only came to be from my father's mother. I can't even remember what he said it was before it was changed. My mom's family wasn't much different in terms of ancestry. To my parents' credit, they have done an awesome job in raising us. I believe that whatever you lacked as a child you will tend to give more to your own children. For example, my dad lacked education; therefore, he stressed education. My mom loves family because she had only a few whole relatives in her life. We, as black people born in America, are bits and pieces of a whole lot of things.

As I was talking with my Dad, whom I love and honor, he told me to leave the past in the past and to start from the present to make something of it now. This was not the first time I had received this advice from him.

I wanted to know where I came from and about the past, so I will know how it affects my future. Without it, I have nothing to share with my kids, and the knowledge of my ancestry could perish with my parents. I wanted to understand why I have been drawn to lustful sin, when I have the love of God in my heart. Why does my pride still get in the way? Why is intimacy and harmony with my wife so difficult at times? Other than my brother, sisters, my mom and my dad, I don't know if I have any full blood relatives alive. I'm afraid to ask. With all of the heartaches and frustrations, I still believe the truth is best. I would rather know the truth than live with an unknown heritage that implies something different.

My parents did their best to raise me right and to prepare me for manhood. I love them deeply and will always be grateful for their love and devotion to our family. Soon they will be celebrating 50 years of marriage, to which all of us are looking forward.

My maternal grandmother on my mother's side was one of the pillars of the Church in the 1940's. She served tirelessly in all aspects of the church ministry. Her love of people and the Church was the legacy that has fed our family. It was this legacy that changed my father's life when he met my mother.

My Dad kept a picture of a young girl in his truck for as long as I can remember. We all wondered who she was, but we never asked. He didn't offer an explanation of who she was, so we thought she was family; she looked unmistakably like my Dad. It wasn't until I was in my teens that I learned that she was my half-sister. My older sister already knew that we had other siblings and threatened to tell us if my Dad did not confront the issue. Dad finally told us the truth about them. At that moment I couldn't have respected him more. It was difficult, but a heavy burden was lifted with the truth. In our efforts not to hurt each other, we lose something critical to our growth and development. God is interested in our needs. He wants to correct them without our contributions. God longs for His people to humble themselves and seek His assistance. He longs for His people to turn from the ideas and the opinions of the flesh.

My father told me that he didn't know what to do, and that is when God began to help him. The Lord taught him through his experiences, both good and bad. This is how he found direction for us. Just as He did with my father, God will supply what Dad couldn't give or teach us; and God will do it in abundance. I may not know the details of my ancestry, but I am assured in the heritage that is mine from God by the way of my parents. He has given them a heart for people, and they have passed that gift of the spirit to my family. We are blessed and highly favored of the Lord!

I've also learned that I cannot ignore or endorse my father's adulterous behavior. There are many things in his life that promoted his behaviors.

We all are responsible for our own actions and reactions. Because we have freedom of choice, we can change, renew, and restore our lives.

I'm glad for Dad because I had been praying for him to give his life to the Lord. The decision to bring all of this to the light was a positive step toward truth. Hiding in the shadows has never been the answer to a life of sin and shame. I thank God that He could start the process of being liberated in Christ Jesus. Hiding can become a convenient habit for good people who love God but don't want to change. We take the power away from our situation by shedding light on it, not by covering it up!

At the end of each chapter I will shed positive light on how that chapter helped me grow and heal in some way.

Like any good parent, God knows us individually so well, and cares for us so much until our test are designed for our perfect-completion. Se'lah.

Chapter 1
"It Is What It Is..."

THE AFFAIR

The learning of my Dad's past infidelities was the beginning of discovering certain things in my life. Those things that were discovered would change my life forever. I felt compelled after that to ask my wife if she had ever cheated on me. I was confident knowing she would say, "No way." I was wrong; she had. I was completely disturbed, undone, hurt, and confused. We were both brought up in the Pentecostal Church where things like that just didn't happen! As Pentecostals, we prided ourselves in being faithful in marriage and chaste in our behavior. I wanted to know who, when, where, why and how? My wife didn't want to tell me; she was told and felt that it would ruin our relationship. I thought to myself--what relationship? I held my tongue because this was the woman I loved, and I didn't want to hurt her.

Not knowing what to do, I went to God to ask Him for guidance. What should I do? Who is this person? I had no idea why this was happening. What I did know was that God was with me, and there was a reason this was going on in my life.

A few days later, while in bed, I told my wife I knew who it was. God had revealed to me that it was Bishop Eugene. She paused for a moment and asked what I was going to do. She wanted to tell me but was afraid because she was told that it would destroy our marriage. I waited. Slowly, she began to tell me how it happened.

Before we were married, we both agreed I would continue to pursue my dream of becoming one of the best professional tennis players in the world. We were young, had no children, and had limited resources. It was costly both financially and personally to travel and compete in the professional tennis events. We were apart a great deal in the beginning. I wanted to bring her with me and would make plans to do that. Then, money would get tight, and I would have to call her and cancel our plans. I hated letting her down.

Cookie (my wife's nickname) would never tell me not to go to the events because it would be like telling me to quit. To become a top, world-ranked, professional tennis player, you have to travel to compete against the other top players. It takes a great deal of sacrifice to achieve that ultimate goal of being your best. Little did I know what I was truly sacrificing in pursuit of my dream.

I guess it had gotten to be too much for her, but she felt she couldn't tell me. She had also established a lifestyle, at home, while I was on the road. Survival can cause a person to do things that ordinarily wouldn't be. Those certain secrets, deceptions, and justifications tend to alter one's better judgment.

I had returned from a tournament one day and was departing for another the next. We had gone out to dinner and had a great time while I was at home. The next day, Cookie saw me off at the airport to my next tournament. Thirteen years later, she would tell me she cried like a baby at the airport when I left. That's when she called Bishop Eugene for consolation and guidance. They met, and that is when the affair began.

Cookie needed help and counseling. The Bishop should have, at this time, told me about my wife's problems. Instead, he took advantage of the situation. It was evident, however, that something was there before that moment. My leaving merely opened up the opportunity for something deeper. But, had I known there was a problem with our marriage, I would have quit the pro tour immediately. I would not have sacrificed the bride of my youth for anything on this earth. Because she didn't confide in me, I wasn't given the opportunity to do something. In my absence, Bishop Eugene stole from me something that I will never have back again.

I believe that my wife had a mixture of emotions, desires, and needs that blurred her vision. She was young, bright, intelligent, afraid, and ultimately made a mistake that got way out of control. We all have some fantasies about being with someone else. For most people who are married and have commitments, it ends there. But for this man and my wife, it was a time to act on what had been desired for a long time.

Their romance had begun long before the affair. Cookie worked part-time for the church, and we were very close to Bishop and his family. As a matter of fact, I always rested in the assurance that they would help her if she needed anything while I was gone. I had known Bishop and his family for as long as I could remember. He was twenty-four years older than Cookie, and both our families knew him well. We were raised in a loving church home where we learned to trust and love.

That trust and love was betrayed by a man who abused his position of authority. He used his resources and time to avail himself to the woman I loved. I also believed that there were other men of God in the church who knew about this, but they didn't have the spiritual backbone to do anything about it. It was like a game to them, knowing they could get away with it and that God would forgive. There were others who knew of the affair, and I consider them participants by not saying or doing anything about it. Their silence makes them an accessory and a facilitator to the crime.

In striving to be obedient to God, it's difficult to know what's right. Pastors are responsible for their congregations. With that responsibility they are also given authority. A serious problem arises when the man of God ceases to be responsible but maintains his authority. In order to be responsible, the man of God has to humbly seek God daily and deeply to constantly lead God's people and not bait them. He must be held accountable to someone honest enough to speak truth and change in his life. If this is not done, in respect to his position, the man becomes greater than the message.

Bishop Eugene possessed all the things a woman wanted. He was charming, polished, and educated. He was a very charismatic man in the pulpit. He had gained respect and power as a national leader in the Church. He was able to call the shots in most of his pursuits. My wife worked for the church which gave him the opportunity to lavish her with needed attention, thus no one would think anything of it. At one point, Cookie told me that Bishop wanted to invest $500 in our nail shop, and she asked if it was okay with me. I told her I guessed so.

He had been a client of hers and wanted to help her with her new enterprise. He said the Lord had laid it on his heart to do this for her. I didn't think much of it at the time. We had always tithed ten percent of our income. We knew the Lord used each of us to help others. However, in hindsight, Bishop was using the money to invest in my bride and not in her business.

I believe it was a mixture of things that were put together by the devil that got out of control. A man or woman is tempted when he or she is drawn (James 1:14). Cookie had confided in the Bishop. He took her under his wing as her counselor. He knew I trusted and loved him. He knew he could trust me, and yet he used his authority and position to fulfill his lust. Satan offered Jesus the whole world if He would bow down and worship him. The Bishop did the same thing with my wife when she became the mistress of one of the most powerful men in Pentecostal Church history.

I understand the lust of the flesh and know that when it comes to women, all men need divine intervention. What man wouldn't want to have his cake and eat it too? It is only by God's grace that we overcome the lust of the eye, the lust of the flesh, and the pride of life where sin originates. I don't believe there are many men who know the word of God like this man. Unfortunately, Bishop used his position to feed his lust of the flesh.

God's Word says that the cares of this world, the deceitfulness of riches, and the desires for other things proves unfruitful (Mark 4:19). In order to be a disciple of God and to know the truth about every situation, we must continue in God's Word (John 8:31-32). Bishop Eugene failed to follow this command, and by doing so he damaged the lives of so many.

I called him, and he agreed to meet with me to discuss my wife and his relationship with her. On one Sunday morning, while attending early morning prayer, he tapped me on my shoulder and invited me to his office. While I was praying that morning, he had contacted my wife and asked her if she had told me anything about them. She told him, "no." She advised him to be honest and to tell the truth about the affair.

I told him how God had revealed the situation to me. He vehemently denied it at first, but finally he admitted to having a sexual relationship with Cookie thirteen years earlier. I told him that the Lord had revealed to me that there were other women too. Again he denied it. He was lying about both my wife and his involvement with other women. At that time, he praised my control and commended my character. What he didn't know was that the Lord had already prepared me for this day. He was protecting me from the things that I would face in the future but weren't ready for yet. God's timing is perfect. Little did I know that my whole ministry would be wrapped around this pain that would not go away.

God gave me an amazing level of peace and love during this time. It was terrible that my pastor had done this evil act, but I felt sorry and ashamed for him. My focus and attention went to my brothers and sisters in that church. As we talked, I felt and comprehended something so helpless. Bishop's need was great, and he was trapped in his transgression.

I gave Bishop a book that he seemed to like. He, in exchange, gave me a book of his own entitled *Just like Jesus* by Max Lucado, which he had signed. He also gave me all of his personal numbers and told me to call if I needed to get in touch with him. He offered to apologize to my wife and me together, but I said no way. This had been humiliating enough. I didn't believe that he was really sorry or remorseful; he was just sorry he had been caught. Before I left, Bishop asked if we would remain members of the church. We had lost a lot of members in the last year. I guess he was not eager to lose any more. What gall he had! He did admit that he had committed adultery with my wife, but he wasn't about to jeopardize his position or bring it to the attention to the church.

We would be leaving the church; however, the critical issue for me was how to do so without causing an eruption. Again, God prepared me ahead of time for this moment. I told Bishop that today would be our last day. I told him to tell the congregation that we were going to help out a youth ministry on the other side of town. The young ministry was called "Life Impact." We were also visiting the Potter's House, where the word of God was fresh. Bishop Eugene thought what we wanted to do was a good idea. He had also mentioned to me that he should have been the one to leave and not us. It sounded good, but he didn't mean it. I told him that he had a responsibility to the people of God first. I felt that those souls needed him, and it would have been worse seeing them dispersed.

For the first time ever, Bishop announced from the pulpit that Brother Glen and Sister Cookie would be leaving the ministry for another youth ministry that was just getting started on the other side of town. Making the break quickly and having it announced from the pulpit would avoid any speculations ahead of time about our departure. The humiliation was great, and the embarrassment was hard to swallow. I thank God that He knows what we really need.

There are specific things for each of us to learn with every new experience. I needed this experience more than my wife because there was so much pride in me. There is such a thin line between confidence and arrogance, wanting to be like God and wanting to be God. It takes maturity to understand that we all have sinned and fallen short. Pain is a positive thing, and what hurts us helps us. As we break, we heal, and when we cover up, we conceal. God is lovingly stretching us beyond legalism, which is the means by which we humans measure ourselves against each other. Instead, God draws us out in love to a rich, dutiful life.

In our brokenness we are made whole, and without having experiences like these we really don't know God. In most cases, we end up talking about ourselves more than glorifying God. God is looking for opportunities to show up and show us who He really is.

When we praise God in the midst of our trying times, it takes away the strength of the need in our lives. When we trust God and not immediately blame Him for the frustration, He is able to change the need to blessing. He is able to show us our real liabilities and not the person that we hold up before others.

The affair will forever be a part of me. The hurt comes and goes. I think in most cases like mine, the person who was wronged has the right to move on. God didn't tell me to do that. God told me to stay with my family. He told me my kids needed a full-time father. He reminded me they were not at fault.

The positive side of this whole experience has been that I had to begin to deal with the pride in my life. I had to learn that it is not about me; it is about God and His purpose for my life. My real struggles come from growing into truth versus growing into what I was taught. Life is a process. We cannot stop with what we learned yesterday. But, the humiliation and shame that have assaulted my manhood will probably always haunt my subconscious. I can fight the truth over and over, but the reality is that God has a plan for me. I am not alone. He is in this with me and my family.

I would like to forever rid myself of the questions that still plague me at times. Did she love him? Did she love him more than she loved me? Would she still rather be with him? Was he better to her than I was? Could I have made a difference had I been home more? How could I have been so far off? What really happened during that time?

I believe that a lot of our patterns of behavior stemmed from our backgrounds. My father was a very proud person. Pride hides itself in proud. Also, I believe there was a lot of promiscuous conduct in Cookie's parents. I wrote them both letters, attempting to explain this revelation that God had shown me about their behaviors. They respected my thoughts, but it was too painful for them to even deal with. God has shown me some serious stuff. They chose not to confront it, but what is done in the dark will come to light.

Because Cookie's parents didn't deal with their demons, they were passed on. When we don't talk about our struggles honestly to someone, we leave a gap or space for the potential for something to get in without our permission. Things that we sweep under the rug don't go away. I don't believe that the affair was our entire fault, but because sexual promiscuity was something that was perpetuated throughout our family, tracts of opportunity for evil manifested. And when we don't deal with our sin, our sin deals with us. Only by being honest with God right where we are can we grow.

None of the affair was against Cookie's will. She consented to this over and over again. I wrestle with the thoughts that I am just as good as he and that I can do what it takes to make it on my own. I've always been a man of action; however, I am hurt. Now I am not so sure of myself. I am not sure of anything.

I really don't want to be where I am. I feel everyone knows what a fool I was. I figure they think yes, you loved God, but it was your fault in some way. A real man wouldn't take this; my pride is now getting in the way. I would rather be right with God than wrong outside of him. How will I go on? I know I will eventually have to face people and their pity. I feel sorry for me too. Where do I go? There is nowhere to hide. There is no peace other than with God. I don't even want God's pity. I want out. I don't want God. God has failed me. It's all too much. I know He is supposed to be my strength and my refuge. His Word is there to protect me from the weak thoughts that seek to destroy me and my family. His Word tells me the truth when the devil comes to whisper lies to me. But is it a lie?

Bishop and my wife must have had long, steamy, lustful showers together after hours and hours of making passionate love. There must have been intimate talks and close exchanges before, during, and after the process. To imagine being in the bed with another woman other than my wife is difficult. It doesn't mean that the desires to do so are not there, but the investment of love is so much greater. The responsibility that I have means so much. For her to cross that line and for him to become that conduit was unreal to me. I become a slave to my thoughts. I've got to get outside of myself! I need to hurt something. I need to know someone or something understands my pain. But what would that really accomplish? I am left alone to wonder while I contemplate their passion at the expense of my pain.

Bishop encouraged and justified his behavior. Bishop probably made me look like someone who didn't care for his wife at all. Because of him being older and wiser, he had more of an advantage over me. I believe Bishop thinks that he has won and that he is better than me.

I questioned why I deserved this. Why should I still be around? God, did you create us for each other? Then why am I in this situation? Why am I the loser? Is this my fault? All of this is not possible, and it cannot be happening to me, but it is. I knew what God's Word says; however, my hurt and shame were about to consume me. I began to think I didn't want to live—death seemed to be the honorable way out. The shame imprisoned me. I didn't know if I could make it. God tells me that if He is for me, He is more than the world and anything that is against me. When I wanted to lose it all, God assured me that He had not given me the spirit of fear but has given me soundness of mind. He has given me love beyond sin and power within weakness. I understood that this is how I can and will make it beyond the affair.

The truth is that I don't know how I'm making it. There were many times when I felt that He was carrying me when I couldn't go on anymore. It was definitely a supernatural thing. God is looking for opportunities in our lives to show up in supernatural ways, so that others can see His supernatural power.

He is supernaturally helping me to forgive, but I can't necessarily forget. I feel that, somehow, I'm not supposed to forget. I am to remember, for therein lies power. When I remember what God has done for me, it's hard to blame, or charge people for their transgressions. When I see how ugly my sin is and realize its deep, dark effects, I'm not so quick to criticize or blame others for their shortcomings. Therefore, I can praise God for this experience because I know He has used it to change me.

I still have difficulty today looking my wife in her eyes. I want too, but when I look into her eyes, she can see into my heart at the most vulnerable part of me. I am a little afraid to give her my heart completely. I really want to try, but I don't want to give anyone that part of me again. This may not be the right thing, but I have justified it to myself as a means of protection. God, you said if I trust you, you would provide and take care of me and my family. But then I think, how could you do this to me? How could she do this to me? I know she enjoyed it. Sometimes I think I can't forgive her.

All the things Bishop could not enjoy in his own wife, he was able to enjoy in others, more specifically mine. It was probably a relief when Bishop's wife was on her menstrual cycle and had PMS. These excuses gave him the opportunity to take what belonged to someone else--all in the name of "God Forgives." I believe Bishop's wife knew about his lifestyle but suffered quietly. She struggled with her own embarrassment, self-denial, and humiliation. She was clearly frustrated and helpless, having to pretend and go along with his evil.

I have got to get this out of me because it has been locked up. I won't feel free until I do. I have walked around feeling that when I leave home, he will be coming in my back door. I think about how committed I was to the church ministry and how willing I was to do whatever was needed. How could Bishop and my wife continue to justify their behavior? I was a joke to them. Their lust was more important. He wasn't a man, and she loved herself more than the truth.

At 46, I can understand the pressures of living and striving to remain faithful to God. It's much easier to live a life of sin, but the results are detrimental. It is a challenge at times, and if it were not for the grace and mercy of God, my life would be a mess. With age comes maturity. I am a lot smarter and more careful than I was at 24. I know more of how to enjoy myself and how to please others. I want to savor the moment and to enjoy and appreciate the memories. Bishop had the pleasure to do all of this. While I was somewhere trying to put two nickels together to make a dime, trying to keep a roof over our heads and gas in our cars to get to work, trying to keep the lights on, what were they doing? It makes no sense to me.

I think about how he talked dirty to her, and how he discredited me, to support his own infidelity. I know she was that "pretty young thing" to him. Remember, I am the older man now. I don't see 19 and 20 year old girls as something to be conquered. They are attractive, but it is wrong, irresponsible and criminal to violate their innocence. Where is the line drawn? What happens when we violate the rules? It appears that you get away with it, but do you get away? I should be able to cheat, too! Why not?

If God doesn't help us, our ideas and sinful natures will destroy anything that would be good about us. My life is a wreck, and without God, I would lose my mind. Why would a person want to go on in my situation? I realize that people have suffered greater losses. I think if I just died, then maybe in my death, I would have some dignity. Everyday, I want to do something about it. It comes with my choleric personality. God created me to be this way. He is going to use this for His glory. I need to get beyond my flesh, but it's my flesh that hurts. It weeps for justice. It wants to go back to a place before the affair happened. My flesh seeks to be protected from exposure. It doesn't want what God wants. It wants to be stable and secure. It wants to be respected and honored.

I am struggling to realize I don't belong to myself. I didn't die for my sins. I am not capable of correcting what happened years ago in the Garden of Eden. Only God can do that, and only God can do this.

Our personal choices can be far from those of God. Somehow, in the midst of our humanity, God helps us make it work for our good and toward His purpose. I am forever blessed by His ever-knowing knowledge of my life. But still I struggle with my flesh on a daily basis. It is a constant battle--the flesh against the spirit. It is one we will lose without our Lord and Savior Jesus Christ.

In this chapter I learned that God's ways are higher than my ways. Is.55:9.

As we seek the Lord, and allow Him a word in edge wise, He promises to deliver us from all our fears. If we respect Him He promises that all of our choices will be the right ones. Psalm.25:12 I respected me, at the time, much more than I respected Him.

Chapter 2
"Being Kind, Over Right, Is Always Better."

THE ANGER AND THE THOUGHTS

I had a really difficult time with anger and frustration after learning about the affair. I found it difficult to avoid the thoughts and mental pictures that fanned destructive flames in my mind. I awoke with thoughts of the affair, carried them with me throughout the day, and struggled with them every night. The thought of being "played," and the bitterness of betrayal was something that was consuming me.

I was like a dead man walking. I felt so lost. I wanted out. I wanted revenge. I thought about how I loved Bishop and his ministry. How could he have done this to me? It still upsets me; yet, I am sure it was within God's plans for me. I see evidence of this truth as the Lord shows me that He will use this experience to help others not to give up on their marriages. I pray that others can learn from our story—our mistakes and our victories.

My first step was to get out of denial. Denial separates us from receiving needed information. The second step for me was to be honest about my feelings, and the third step was for me to face my fears. But the devil doesn't want us to face our fears. He would rather we wish them away. His deception is subtle and appealing. Our self-centered greed for more is easy fodder for Satan's lusty appetite. He tells us that God is not enough, when God has promised us more than enough for all we face. He makes the truth look like a lie and a lie look like the truth. He dresses up the outward appearances and perfumes our sins, but he never shows us the need for a bath and deodorant. He won't mention the daily maintenance needed to sustain good spiritual hygiene. Instead, he paints a picture of what we deserve, and in the process we mutter and complain about almost everything. My anger and thoughts were completely out of control, mostly because we live and breathe in a society that breeds negativity. People, in general, are misery loving company. Few people are genuinely happy with themselves or the success of others. I didn't feel cared for. I was angry and mad, and there was nothing around me that spoke differently.

Satan's ways are so much like God, but so far from God all at the same time. Satan is an imitation that can never be the real thing. He hates being second to what was always the One and only. Satan's constant job is to harass, accuse, frustrate, and erase the presence and relevance of God in the lives of God's people. It's frustrating to me because I get confused. When I'm in my flesh, it looks like God, but after getting back in the Word, I realize that I wasn't walking in the Spirit. Anger rests in the bosom of a fool, but in the Spirit anger cannot rest!

Because of my insecurity, I am numb. I feel nothing. I know this attack is artificial, but it seems real. My hurt and my shame seem to be more than I can handle. I only hope and pray for one more day to be better than this day. I was raised to take pride in my family and to work hard for what belongs to me. Now I feel embarrassed. God's Word assures me that this pain will pass, but it's impossible to see beyond the pain I live with daily. Where there is a struggle, there is a promise that the pain will end for me.

I learned that nothing belongs to me. 1 Chronicles 29:11-12:

Everything in the heaven and earth is yours, O Lord and this is your kingdom. We adore you as being in control of everything. Riches and honor come from you alone and you are ruler of all mankind; your hand controls power and might and it is at your discretion that men are made great and given strength. (Living Bible)

Chapter 3
"I Came Not To Be Served, but To Serve."

DAVID AND URIAH

The story of David and Uriah is one of trust, respect and servitude. David was given authority and position to move a nation of people into their next level of anointing. For this authority, he was duly respected. King David had favor, wisdom and good common sense; he was also a mighty warrior. King David had good looks and charm. He was the full package. Where Saul had killed thousands, David had killed tens of thousands. King David was a man of greatness and was anointed by God to lead his nation. Uriah greatly loved and respected his commanding officer.

Uriah was one of many servants; however, he wasn't an expendable front line solider in King David's army. Uriah held a position in the army that normally kept him from the front lines. When Uriah was given the opportunity by King David to lay with his wife while the fighting continued, Uriah refused. Uriah was concerned about those at war. He didn't feel it was right for him to enjoy the pleasure of his wife while other's lives were in jeopardy. Clearly, Uriah was a man of strength and character. Uriah's love and commitment to his family and the mission of his king made it difficult for King David to cover his sin. Had Uriah been lazy or irresponsible, rather than selfless and dedicated, King David would have had an easier time of it.

King David went to God with the desire of his heart, but God wouldn't sanction the desire. God didn't tell King David what he wanted to hear. Because King David's heart wasn't set in obedience to God, King David didn't understand that everything he encountered in his life was by God's design. It was the same for me and Bishop.

When we try to alter God's plans for our lives, to fit what is pleasurable for our own, trouble is always lurking in the shadows. Because we don't see its imminent danger, we flirt with it like a cat toys with a mouse. We are unaware the devil, in a flash, turns the mouse into an oversized pit bull.

I served Bishop and the church's ministry with conviction. Bishop held me in his confidence and sought my support in asking the Lord for guidance and blessing. I respected Bishop, and so did many people across the country. He was a national evangelist prior to becoming our full-time pastor. Bishop was well-groomed for the position with a deep heritage of pastors in his family. He had everything and all of the things I didn't have. I loved him and put myself on the front line for the ministry.

The flow of the service, the praise, the worship, and the choir were all integral parts of the worship by which spiritual success was facilitated. It all worked together to bring the delivery of the word. Bishop often gave thanks for the prayer ministries, for the spiritual successes of our Sunday morning church services. I was so proud to be part of that ministry and to tell people that my pastor was the Bishop. Like King David, Bishop had a heart for God, but also like King David, Bishop was distracted by the desires of his heart.

With the power of God comes the responsibility of team work. We are called to be a community of believers and to surround ourselves with those who love God and who are consistent in our relationship with God. We may not like everything about our fellow believers, but in our hearts, we know that they are honest. In our diversity lies our creativity, insight, and strength. Diversity builds a strong base, or foundation of truth. The truth is not always pleasurable, but it is enduring. As we grow through our differences and honestly share, we become unstoppable. It is by way of the community that God holds us accountable for our behavior. Some-times the truth hurts, but it's needed. Proverbs 27:6 says, "Faithful are the wounds of a friend, but kisses of an enemy are deceitful." Bishop Eugene wasn't only my pastor--he was my friend.

But a friend influenced by the devil is an incalculable evil. It is like a person that has no control over his bodily fluids, or a teenager that continues to urinate on himself. Without some kind of serious medical attention, you will have an uncontrollable problem. When sin is finished, it brings forth death.

Unfortunately, in some cases there seems to be a hidden code in minis-try by which like-minded people are placed in strategic positions within the ministry. This serves to homogenize the direction of the ministry through the path of least resistance. This hidden code hurts the entire ministry. It is our unique differences that see a vital part of God's means to challenge ministries and to bring about growth and spiritual maturity. The people in these positions are good people who can be very helpful; however, they might not be the right people to challenge the whole ministry. They might not be the right people to take the ministry to the next level with God. Every person needs someone who will hold them accountable for their actions. King David lacked accountability, as did Bishop.

It is an extremely evil thing to get wrapped up in justifying your behavior, good or bad. It's a waste of time, and it facilitates a great need, or trouble, and no one wins. To expose our pain eventually strengthens our relationships and brings clarity to a weaker, more useless scenario. To make excuses or have self-pity helps us to accomplish nothing. We all make mistakes, and we all have some successes, so what is it all about? What is the big deal? God is God alone. All the rest of us are equal--equal as it relates to respect, needs, love, attention, and responsibility. We lose this when we start to judge things and look to others as our source.

I don't believe that the relationship between Bishop and my wife ever had to become what it was, but it did. Not to confess your faults or admit your arrogance is a betrayal in the deepest and worst sense because it won't stop there. It keeps on growing!

There were plenty of people around Bishop, but no one loved him enough to honestly talk to him about what he was doing. Just as Uriah respected King David, I respected the position and authority of Bishop. I wasn't a "Yes Sir" type of man, but I did respect his ministry and vision. I was loyal to my church and faithful in my time, talents, and giving.

God was so faithful to me; I was afraid not to be faithful in return. Like Uriah, I also had a beautiful wife who caught the eye of one in authority. Uriah's beautiful wife cost him his life. He was innocent, honest, hard-working and a man striving to honor his king and his family. King David took advantage of that and eventually murdered Uriah. I don't believe Uriah ever saw it coming. I don't think he even expected it. I know I didn't. I wonder what Uriah would have done had he known?

I was not shocked that things like my wife's affair happen. I was shocked to be the last one to find out. I was shocked to learn this happened in my family. How could this have happened when I have sought to serve God with such an earnest heart? How did this get past the awesome foreknowledge of God? Obviously, it is impossible for God not to know, but it confused me at times. I was in a strange place. This was to me as death was to Uriah. The betrayal of Bishop and my wife threatened to take my life and my family. The devil wants our soul, and he will use any means necessary to get it.

When you are hurt, you want to blame God and everyone else. His ways are not our ways. His ways are perfect. God wanted me to be whole and equipped for life through this experience much like the butterfly and the cocoon. God is preparing us now for tomorrow's difficulties. If we love our life we must be willing to lose it and to those who are willing to lose their life will gain it. I really didn't want to live. The embarrassment was too great. Everything that I had been taught was violated! I felt like I had nobody and nothing to call my own. I didn't know what was real anymore.

Like King David, Bishop was God's anointed. God's Word says to "Touch not his anointed and to do His prophet no harm." King David was wrong, but God is always right. What hurts us the most will end up helping us and others. It will eventually help you as a person, if you can get through.

King David committed adultery with Uriah's wife and then sought to cover it up. Adding misery to trouble, King David then kills Uriah. Even after Uriah's death, God's plan for the ministry to continue was so important that God reached over into our dispensation of grace to pardon King David's life that it might be spared. I had every opportunity to ruin Bishop by legally taking him to court and winning. There were ministers who were in jail for much less than what he did to us. People advised me to do this, but God said not to touch him. I wanted to. I wanted to physically wreak havoc in the church and sit and wait for Bishop to appear just to see what he would do. He couldn't have hurt me because I was already dead. I would have had my revenge, but also probably would have lost my life. Such disobedience results in death. In obedience, I have by grace, chosen life for myself and my family.

God uses our situations to promote a higher consciousness of Himself. What the devil means for evil, God uses for good. Behind al of the devil's messes is a message of God's unconditional love for us. He is not waiting for us to do right to love us. He loves us anyway and without conditions. He is forever waiting with His arms stretched wide.

Even when Cain had unjustifiably killed his brother, God said if anyone harmed Cain that He would punish them sevenfold. It is really not who is right; it's what's right. Both can be different for each person. What is right and who is right can only be discerned in the heart. Only God can help us to understand the difference. Our one-on-one relationship with Him is our greatest and most imperative necessity.

There will be places and times in our lives where no one will be able to help us but Him--not your religion, money, good looks, family ties, education background, your 401k plan, your influences or anything else can help you. God's love and peace are supreme. God's approval in our lives makes us the head not the tail, above not beneath. God's presence in our lives gives us the confidence and security that everything is under His control. Even being betrayed and losing everything that I thought was important to me was a creation made by God for a needed purpose. Isaiah 45:7 proves my point. It says, "I (the Lord) form the light and create darkness, I make peace and create evil, I the Lord do all these things."

Light and darkness are the same to God. Peace and evil were created by Him. Our evil and our good are the same to Him. So what's wrong?

To fight God is never the right approach. To blame, complain, and attack God is always the wrong thing. I love God; however, I don't fully understand love. I need help figuring out the truth about myself before I can make sense of life. "Why me?" is a question that we all ask God at different times. The answer is for His glory and if not you, then who? God's purpose for our life is to serve and to save the lost. Who else would be willing? Why not you? Think about the honor that comes to those whom God can use for His glory.

Bishop Jakes preached a powerful message entitled, "Nothing Just Happens".

It was an awesome sermon that dealt with God's divine plan for our lives. The timing was perfect for me, because I felt that God had completely forgotten about me, or that He was totally out of His mind. If God closes a door, always look for a window.

Chapter 4
"God Is Not Fair, Because if He Was It Would Have Been Over a Long Time Ago!"

WHEN THE DAMAGE HAS BEEN DONE

When one's trust has been violated due to an affair, the damage is devastating. The mental damage is initially irreparable, especially when a couple has been committed to each other. The trust has been severed. For me, I had to deal with the fact of I wasn't "The Man" anymore. My main feeling was pride. It was the way I felt and still feel. I think it's natural to feel this way. It takes God and a lot of fortitude to stay straight in a relationship. It's difficult fighting the desires, and we all make mistakes. The path of righteousness is no easy one, even with God in your life.

To know that someone else made love to my wife--the one that God gave me to love and cherish--was ruinous and demoralizing. It was only by God's grace and mercy that I have been allowed to make it. It has been a process of inches and feet, putting one foot in front of the other and continuing on in hope. Nothing will take away what has happened to me. There is neither distance nor any tonic that will wash away the pain. Only God can heal me.

It is only through such an experience that we come to know the amazing grace of God and the reality of a certain destiny attached to our pain. It is in this knowledge where we can find comfort. Inevitably, our minds slide into wanting revenge or to run away, but there is no escape.

There are haunting reminders every single day of betrayal and pain, which the devil uses to draw us away from God. He whispers, "You don't have to take this. You can start over. Just get rid of the problem." Without God, the devil's appealing words can take root and lead us astray.

When fear surrounds you like a gang on a mission, and insecurity causes you to hold your breath because you are so afraid, only God can supply your need. He has a plan, a way of escape and hope for your betrayal. His Word always gives us the direction if we follow His plan. We must learn to follow before we will ever become a good leader. Thank God for Jesus Christ, who led the way and became the example, and showed us the way.

Everything about Jesus' life was exemplary. He came to His own, and His own received Him not. He had compassion on the needy and spent time with those that were poor. He didn't break the law, and when He was accused and mistreated, He didn't blame life. When He could have spoken out for what was right, He waived His rights. For you and I, He said not a mumbling word to prove that His love for us would always be greater than our love for Him.

YOU CHOSE THE WAY YOU THINK, AND AS YOU THINK, SO ARE YOU. THINK ON THESE THINGS. (Philippians 4:8). The things that are of a positive nature, and of a truthful and honest concern, and that is pure and that gives others the benefit of the doubt. Character respects the needs in others, and is not so concerned about one's neediness.

Chapter 5
"I Don't Need Anybody, I Need Everybody."

WHEN LOVE DIDN'T HAVE
ANYTHING TO DO WITH IT

We often feel we can do things and expect no repercussions from our actions.

We feel that because God has forgiven us, we are covered. The love that I have for my wife is pretty incredible. I wouldn't want to live my life without her, but I could. The pain can be so great in a person's life that no amount of love can keep it all together. The possibility of failure to keep our marriage together is a nagging fear. As we seek God's face, He shows us our real selves mercifully, a little at a time. In revealing our sinful nature, He helps us to self-correct the problems we encounter. By doing this, God enables us to gain strength over what we fear. With strength over our fears, the sin that clings to us slowly but surely loses its grip in our lives.

Fear in the secular world pushes some over the edge to suicide, murder, or both. Without God's intervention and His allowing us to see our destiny more clearly, our fear will kill our faith in God. In Romans 5:3-5, Paul writes

> . . . we also rejoice in our sufferings, because we know that suffering brings about perseverance; perseverance brings about character; and character, hope. And hope does not disappoint us, because God has poured out his love into our hearts by the Holy Spirit, whom he has given us.

We are free from fear, and we are thankful for our troubles, which have served to increase our faith. This is God's design for us and His plan for our lives. Experience is a great teacher, and with each other we have come to know more fully that there is nothing that can overwhelm us when we have Christ as our protector and our advocate. To live is to glorify God and in

Him our flesh is crucified. Once the world can quit seeing us, then it can begin to see God. Our own glory and self-recognition along with our pride means more to us than who God is in our lives. We must be humbled and our pride stripped before we can understand the way we really are. Only then can we walk in faith and believe God beyond our circumstances.

The movie *What's Love Got to Do with It* portrays Tina Turner's very abusive relationship with her husband, Ike. Ike used and disrespected her; however, Tina loved and respected him dearly. He was everything but a man. A real man would never put his hands on a woman to hurt her. This would be the difference for some men who are not taught this. My point is that there is not enough water in the Pacific Ocean to remain in a relationship with a woman who feels I cannot live without her. When you cheat and disrespect a person you love, and your excuse is, "I made a mistake," you might find yourself alone.

We all can do badly by ourselves. So if you have found that one person that completes you, be honest with them even if it hurts. Everyone makes mistakes, but when those mistakes become abusive and disrespectful, you could end up losing the best friend you have ever known.

I don't even know if it's possible to know if you have a true friend until something bad happens. A real friend will be honest and tell you the truth. A real friend is not perfect. A friend is one that you confide in. There must be sensitivity in the relationship as delicate as a surgeon's use of a scalpel. When you care about someone, it's important that you are concerned about their needs and their well-being.

Bishop Eugene didn't love me. He didn't care about me nearly as much as he cared about himself. I was nobody to him—love had nothing to do with it. As for my wife, the blind was leading the blind. Where was the love between them? I thank God that His love is for real, and He proved it by giving His life for us. When love didn't have anything to do with it, He died for us. He broke all the rules for us so that we could do the same for each other.

I was writing out of some real pain here. If you are here in your pain you need to read the whole 11th chapter of Hebrews. Without faith it is impossible to please God.

When we finally give up, and when it's impossible for us, that's when God gets the chance to SHOW OUT!!! READ THE REST OF THE STORY! WE WIN! :)

Chapter 6
"What Didn't Kill You Will Make You Stronger!"

HOW DID IT AFFECT THE CHILDREN?

There is a lot my children don't know and don't understand. They know a little about what happened, but they are unclear about the details. God has truly covered them, but eventually they should know and learn from our experiences. What has happened to me and Cookie will help my children. It will bring some understanding of how difficult things have been for us. Through this, my children will understand the greatness of God, even in the midst of our storm. Most families have challenges and problems, and our problems are no different. At times, my wife and I bump heads and disagree. This is simply a part of life. What is great about our situation is that we are still together. My children see their friends' parents divorced and other family members' parents moving on to other relationships. The children of these relationships are suffering because of their parent's choices. Kids are not dumb; they know more than we imagine. As in our lives, these experiences can make them stronger and tougher individuals.

I think it is very important for us to constantly evaluate where we are. In the midst of everything, we must make sure that our children know that they are special and never the cause of our frustration. We should make sure our children know that our disagreements are never a reflection of our love for them. It is critical that our children understand this. We have moved them from church to church and in and out of relationships with people they love. We need to reaffirm that they are chosen and unique in the eyes of our awesome Lord and Savior Jesus Christ. This is extremely essential and draws us closer as a family.

Our children are ages 17, 15, and 13, and we are so proud of them. They are all honor students and all love the Lord. This is an incredible blessing. I am extremely grateful to God for the understanding He has given them. I see God's work in them, and I am amazed by the wisdom and truth He speaks through them. I believe we, as a family, have been challenged. We have been so abundantly blessed by God. Sometimes it seems like we're treading water in the middle of the ocean, but as long as God is with us, we will make it and will continue to grow.

Trying to find the balance of how honest to be with the children has been difficult. I have struggled with the discernment to know how much is too much to say or do. Have I given them a truly good experience, or has it been a nightmare for them? As a father, knowing what to do or not to do can be trial by error. Honestly, most of the time I don't really know what to do. This keeps me humbly on my knees. If the Lord doesn't help me, I will sink. I have not found many people or books who could guide me beyond the generic in terms of dealing with this life issue. Not finding help has forced me to go to God, which is exactly by His design. We were created for this very purpose to have communion with God. You are forced to know him better, as He allows you to understand "you" as a person with all your needs and vulnerabilities.

Our children already know that God has a certain plan for their lives. They also know that we were chosen to be their parents. Win or lose, God's design is woven in all of the events that take place in our lives. Our children are typical children; they fuss and argue and make wrong decisions. They are also blessed and highly favored; they are smart and exceptionally gifted! This is why the Bible tells us to train them in the right way. They are trying to find their way by fitting in and establishing their own identity. They have their own ambitions and their own drives. It is important for us as parents to let our children have their own hopes and dreams and not to push them into something we couldn't attain on our own on them.

In the midst of the ordeal with the Bishop and my wife, God mercifully covered the children and me. He allowed things to develop in pieces so the pain would be dealt with in manageable portions. We were not devastated or overwhelmed. He truly does not give us more than we can handle. "When the devil would come like a flood, the spirit of the Lord would lift up a standard against him." (Isaiah 59:19) Our flesh cries out for comfort and relief, but without the pain, we miss some of the message.

I think the children will be challenged more as they mature to handle different challenges. This experience will help them and humble them. To even think that I could possibly not be their biological father is devastating. I believe they are mine, but there is no way of being absolutely sure other than DNA testing. They will forever be mine. The tests are in our loving and eternal commitment to each other. It is not their fault that their mom and I had some problems. They need a Mother and Father. By God's grace and mercy, that is exactly what we will be.

MY KID'S MEAN SO MUCH TO ME. THEY GIVE ME AN IN-SIGHT INTO HOW MUCH GOD LOVE'S ME. KNOWING GOD'S LOVE IS REALLY A SPECIAL THING, AND A THING THAT WE MUST CONSTANTLY GO TO GOD ABOUT, IN PRAYER. IT WAS AMAZING HOW GOD TAUGHT ME THROUGH MY KID'S AND THEN SHOWED ME HIS LOVE FOR US THROUGH THEM.

YOU CAN'T GET THIS WITHOUT GETTING THAT!

Chapter 7
"Exposed, Or Covered?"

LIFE TODAY SHOW WITH JAMES AND BETTY ROBISON

Humiliated and in pain, I was looking everywhere for support and answers. I wanted to know if my marriage was salvageable. I knew we needed help.

One day while I was at work, I turned on the television and heard James and Betty Robison talking on their Christian television show about relationships. They were dealing with hard, cold facts and real issues. It soothed my pain a bit to know that others struggled with some of the same issues my wife and I had. I called in with a prayer request and asked how I could be part of the studio audience. I wanted to be closer to the discussion. The lady who counseled me took down some information and told me she would call me back, and she did. She asked if my wife and I would consider being a feature couple on the show.

I called my wife and told her that "Life Today" was considering having us on the show. I asked if she was interested, she was and wanted to hear more details of the show. After talking it over, she and I both knew that this was a national television show, meaning everyone would know our business. This would include our friends and family. Revealing our problems could hinder our relationship with them.

We considered that friends might feel uncomfortable around us after the show. Some of the parents of our children's friends might not want their children hanging around our house anymore. Our own families might desert us. Weighing all of these things, we decided to go on the show for two reasons. One, the Lord could use our situation as a witness to others who were going through some of the same things. We were both looking for inner healing and understanding of what went wrong in our marriage. We felt that this was an opportunity to learn from other couples featured on the program. Second, we wanted James and Betty to share their wisdom with us and to pray for us.

Before my wife agreed to be on the show, she wanted me to know the whole truth. Until this time, I had believed what God had revealed and confirmed to me. I had also believed what Bishop had told me. I believed they had only one sexual encounter thirteen years ago. My wife finally told me the affair lasted for more than four years. I was devastated all over again. God had revealed to me that it happened, but He didn't tell me that it went on for more than four years. Until this time, God had protected me from too much information at once. But then came the real defining moment.

Two of our precious children were conceived during the affair and could possibly have been born of the Bishop and not me. Could there be anything more horrific than this? How could we continue in life together with such pain? God's timing is perfect. He had prepared me for this, even though I felt abandoned and alone in my rage and grief. The hurt I felt was unbearable. What could I have possibly done to deserve this pain? I wanted out. I wanted to disappear and then reappear with everything back to normal, before I learned of the affair. It didn't seem real to me. I was numb and pierced at the same time. I needed help.

I walked up and down the street that night and cried. I hated her and him. I was a mess. I got into my car and drove to the church. I told the Lord I wasn't leaving until He helped me that night. God spoke to me and said

> Glen, I understand your anger. You have my permission to move on and start your life somewhere else. There is a purpose in all that I am doing in your life. My glory will minister to others in a powerful way if you are willing to trust me. There is a connection between your pain and your destiny. Your struggle will reveal your fears. Your faith will defeat them. The arm of the flesh will try its best to work out what only I can do in your life. Your need for control has cost you a great deal. Trust in me. I know parts of you that you don't even know exist. Glen, I want more for you than you can imagine. Whatever decision you make, I am going to be there with you. While you're making your decision, think about this. Remember when you weren't always doing what was right. I didn't judge you. I didn't give up on you. I just kept loving you and feeding you my Word. When you needed affirmation

and action, I provided it for you. The love that I have for you is unmatchable and beyond what you can comprehend. Now you are free to make your decision . . . and remember whatever decision you make I will always be there for you. I love you with an everlasting love.

Jesus Christ

I remember weeping so heavily that the carpet near the altar of the church was soaked. When nothing else could help, love lifted me. Even with another deep wound and fresh pain, God gave me the peace and confidence to continue with our plans to appear on the show with the Robisons. While we are living our lives, we believe we can do and be whatever we want; however, this is not true. It is a lie to think you can be whatever you want to be in life. You can only be what God plans for you to be. You will be where you are in the destiny that God had planned for us before the world began. God also knew about the thousands of people who would be helped because we were willing to obey and endure for His glory.

The taping sessions were actually four shows in one day. They all featured couples in their particular struggles. The logistics of the production was interesting as were the stories of each couple. The common thread that bound us couples was the lack of communication in each relationship. It was obvious by the end of taping that we all could have avoided a great deal of the trauma in our lives with some honest communication. We were later told that our show had one of the highest ratings and that many people were blessed by our message.

Avoiding thorny issues doesn't make for a smooth road in life. We need to use discretion and tact. We also need to face these issues together with our spouse rather than avoid them. Problems don't just go away. When weeds pop up in the garden, the gardener doesn't prune them as he does intended harvest. Pruning only makes the plants flourish. Weeds must be taken out by the root in order to rid them from the garden. It is much easier to wait, put off, or even avoid certain uncomfortable situations or conflicts. We need to face up to problems that could destroy us or possibly liberate us eternally. Sin takes root in the unresolved issues of our relationships. God is the gardener. It is by His hand that we are pruned. The weeds are removed from our lives, so that He may be glorified. His grace reconciles us. He leads us to repentance or restoration and, by this, our faith. He renews and strengthens. I am so glad I found out about the affair. I was struggling with something that I could not see, taste, or touch. The power of my struggle was enormous. When a person can't see his struggle, he can't help himself. That was me. Once I was able to see God's love, He brought tears of gratitude to my eyes. He has always been with me. God has proven to be ever faithful.

The experience on the Robison's show clearly showed us that sins must come to a place of repentance. Sins of omission and commission lead to disastrous situations. We can justify it as much as we want, but until we come clean, we will never truly be set free from our past. Time will heal the pain, and our experiences are the cement that stabilizes our Christian walk and blesses others.

After the show, my wife and I had several calls and letters across the country expressing their thanks and appreciations. There were some people in the church who felt uncomfortable about the program. They were taught to cover up and hide what couldn't be explained. So many of our members were leaving the church and going to the Potter's House. We were not being fed the Word. We were struggling under a fallen leader who would not step down or openly repent his ways. There were others who wrote who thought Bishop Eugene should have been imprisoned and exposed. I appreciated their concern and compassion, and I explained that action was not the right thing for me and my family. Pride is so destructive. It is a weed with a deep root. Not exposing Bishop Eugene helped me to pull up that deep wicked root of pride. It was painful, but necessary.

PRIDE IS ONE OF THE SCARIEST EVILS KNOWN TO MAN. IT'S TASTELESS, ODORLESS, OFTEN UNNOTICED, AND HARD TO PROVE WRONG. IN MANY CASES IT GOES UN DETECT-ED, AND IS LOOKED OVER. IT IS AN EVIL THAT GOD HATES. I THANK GOD THAT IT WAS EXPOSED IN ME, AND DEALT WITH HEAD ON!

Chapter 8
"The Man, the Vision."

BISHOP T.D. JAKES AND THE POTTER'S HOUSE

The teachings that we received at the Potter's House were everything that we didn't receive from our Church with Bishop Eugene. It was an opportunity to exhale and hear God clearly; there was no judging, pretending, or defending. I felt love that stemmed from a relationship with God and obedience to His Word. This atmosphere provided a chance to heal and realize that God gives gifts and talents naturally, but our growth and development come through honest repentance. Repentance breeds clarity to see yourself rightly before God. I was so unclear and confused that I didn't know which way was up, and confusion is not of God. I thought I knew myself, but I didn't. The pastor of the Potter's House, Bishop T.D. Jakes, has been one of the greatest blessings in my life. God led me and my family to his church. He has worked through Bishop Jakes in a powerful way. Our old church had serious damage. Bishop Jakes helped us to move forward through the Word of God. It seemed that everyone was stirred up by our revelations. Others, from the old church, began to recount similar experiences with Bishop Eugene. Some told us our experience had ministered to their marriages. The reactions were as diverse as the people.

We had a meeting with Bishop and Serita Jakes about how to handle this situation. Bishop Jakes led us through discussion with discerning questions and allowed us to air out our frustrations and pain. His ability to listen equaled his ability to deliver God's Word. Though we had great pain and disappointment, we felt Bishop Jakes helped bring us to a place of peace. He led us to face the truth.

I was in shock and disbelief after learning of the affair. I still am. I never saw it coming. Having grown up in the Church, I never imagined anything like this would happen to me. I surely never thought it would happen without some sort of "heads up" from God.

Bishop Jakes taught me that to make a mistake is part of everyone's life. We just need to learn from the experience and get back up in the saddle.

We are all damaged goods. We need God's help to be real rather than a facade. We must deal with issues head on and not ignore them. To be tempted and distracted at times is all part of living a godly life. We must know God by coming to church, studying His word, and worshiping Him, not the idea of Him. This was an opportunity to welcome God into my life more fully and to allow Him to show me the idols I had unintentionally put in His place. This is our constant struggle with life. It is not that God doesn't want us to have things in life. It is that He doesn't want things to have us. He wants us to trust what He promised to us. He knew us before we were yet formed in our mother's womb. Through the word of God, Bishop Jakes taught us the need we have for God in our lives. Through our pain and sin, we were led to the Lord. We were brought back to Him in mercy, forgiveness, and blessing.

Bishop Jakes preached a particularly meaningful message one Sunday entitled "Life is Not Against You." When we are at the end of our rope, and we have done all we know to do, God is still there with us with the answer. He is not there just waiting for us to mess up so He can strike us down with lightning. It is here that we find Him. We will always be tempted and will often fall. Our constant prayer should be that our faith does not fail us so that we continue to get back up, knowing that we are the righteousness of God, knowing that if we confess our sins, He is faithful and just to forgive us our sins and cleanse us from all unrighteousness (1 John 1:9).

With the passing of time, I have realized the biggest challenge for me has been, and still is, fear. My idol of having control has been controlling me. I want to be the master of my life and the life of my family. This need for control comes out of fear and clearly lack of trust in the Lord. I fear that this all might happen again. I would be immobilized with fear if it weren't for the Lord, His Word, and His spirit. These things give me peace and faith.

The love, understanding, and wisdom Bishop Jakes brought to our situation have bridged a very rough river for me and my family. The gift of faith sustains me and has kept me in the church--the one place where I find nurture and strength. Apart from God, I can do nothing. Eternal life starts when we become Christians and grow in grace with the encouragement of other believers.

The letter of the law kills us, but the Spirit gives us life. At first, we see in a mirror dimly. When we add precept upon precept and line upon line, we see clearly. It all begins to make sense. For we exult in our tribulations, knowing that tribulation brings about perseverance; perseverance brings about proven character; proven character brings about hope; and hope does not disappoint. It is the love of God that has been poured out within our hearts through the Holy Spirit who was given to us (Roman 5:3-5).

Bishop and Serita Jakes and the Potter's House ministries have been a great source of strength, direction, and nourishment for the souls of me and my family. The Potter's House will always be home for us. The presence of the Lord dwells in that place. Bishop Jakes' word is a sincere, fresh, and honest flow from the throne of heaven. It is not sugar-coated, but it is love-filled. There is a difference. That love mixed with being real is what kept me going on to see what God had for me the next day. And now I know I can make it, when back then I thought I didn't have hope or a chance to go on.

Chapter 9
"For Those That Love Their Lives, They Will Lose It."

GROWING PAINS, PURPOSE, AND GOD'S WILL FOR OUR LIVES

There are insidious thoughts that creep into our minds from our environment. Things that happen at work, something that someone said, or a slight by a loved one are all common things that can open the door of our minds to Satan. These subtle deceits can slowly move us away from God and into the world of idols, namely control. This is what happened to my wife. She was so involved in the church's structure that it was difficult to separate what was right from what was religious. The Bible talks about having a form of godliness and being transformed by the renewing of our minds so that we might be able to prove what is the perfect will of God. Discernment comes out of this renewing of the mind. Otherwise, we are just going by the book. When we get sidetracked, and when we allow our service to God to become more important than our relationship with Him, it is easy to rationalize our actions. We rationalize what we are doing is good and that it is right.

Certain service might be good, but they might not be good for you. The devil is not going to tempt you with the obvious. He will tempt us in areas with which we have the most difficulty. He will tempt us where we are the weakest.

Potiphar's wife wanted Joseph and made that wish very clear. I believe that it was in this area that Satan thought he could most easily break Joseph's steadfast submission to God. God didn't fail Joseph, even when he suffered as a result of the denial of his flesh. Joseph called on the Lord in his act of obedience, and God did not abandon him. Joseph was alert to the possibility of temptation. He was prepared by God to act in accordance with His will. We are never tempted beyond the capacity of God to deliver us. However, we must be watchful, and we must seek renewal of spirit continually. We don't get filled up on Sunday faith that will last until next Sunday. It is a daily struggle that is fought with daily prayer and communion with God.

I am limited, frail and sinful. God is all-powered and true. He is the God who looks out for our best interests in all things, even when they initially are bad. He promises that all things work together for good for those who love Him (Romans 8:28). In life, we must read the fine print and pay attention. It is in the lapses that the devil is waiting to snag us with doubt and self-importance. We take control and forget about God.

I wanted out. I wanted the pain to stop. I wanted to be rid of the battle. My faith had shrunk to an all-time low, and God's purpose for my life was a lost vision for me. My situation was bad, but it was for a greater good. Sometimes our experiences are not about us at all. They are sharpening us to help others to know God better. It is through our travail that the power of God is proven and revealed to others. God wants to trust us. He wants to multiply our blessings. He wants to see us be fruitful, just like he did with Job. Can God use us to bring glory to Him? Yes. It is in our weakness that we are made strong. Our flaws humble us and keep us on our knees. God's strength is made perfect in our weakness, and His grace is sufficient and supports us in our vulnerable moments. Our weakness helps us to be sensitive and compassionate to the needs of others so that we do not become proud and hardened. We must trust God in the midst of our pain and believe that He will complete His work in us.

Also, difficult as it may be, we must maintain trust in our human relationships as well. When my parents told me they were going to do something for me, I believed them. If I had not, it would have hurt them. Lack of trust is far more hurtful than many of the things for which we condemn others. We judge others far too much. We don't know the Word of God well enough to make good decisions. The Bible says, "For hope that is seen is not hope at all. For what a person sees they don't have to hope for." (Romans 8:24) When we stop seeing through the eyes of the ordinary, we start to see the miraculous.

The miraculous is worked out through our weaknesses and God's strength. When it's all about you, He's not there. If it's not about God, then it's not about anything. His presence is the most important thing. Without Him, a number of things can go wrong or get off track. It's about knowing that He is in control. We must be consistent and faithful to God in order to see it correctly in the Spirit. When it's about you, the true meaning gets lost.

Once we start to exercise our faith beyond our pain, we will see that there has been so many more who have suffered. There have been so many who have labored against sin and so many who have suffered for the glory of God. If we get beyond our flesh for a moment, we see that without pain we are ill-prepared for life.

There are others coming behind us for whom we are laying a path. Through our walk, God is planting seeds in the lives of those we encounter each day. We may not see it coming to fruition, but we must trust that God will use us just the same as He has used others to glorify His kingdom. We are surprised at what befalls us, and we call out to God. Doesn't He see what is happening? He should make it better. He should remove that which causes us pain. What we realize with experience and knowledge is that He has designed all that comes to us since the foundation of the Earth. He has already provided for whatever situation we encounter. He loves us enough to bring challenges into our lives, to sharpen and mature us, and to bring us closer to Him.

You see, I had never had anything tough like this in my life. I had no real difficult challenges that I could say, "If it not been for God I wouldn't have made it." God had protected me so well until most of my life that my testimony was more about me than it was about Him. My religious behavior and naivety toward life caused me to be superficial and self-righteous. Without a test in your life, you really don't have a testimony.

Will we leave Him, because we don't understand? Will we lose hope because things are difficult and uncomfortable? Our lives are meant to be lived in order to bring others to Christ. The disciples all died horrible deaths for the glory of God. What He asks of us is comparatively minimal. The road set before me with my wife is designed by God. The road is to be walked faithfully to the glory of God. He loves us. He has a purpose for every problem. All things are possible through Him.

I feel I owe an apology to God and all those He has brought into my life. I didn't handle the situation as I would have liked. I praise God for seeing in my heart and for not judging me for my actions. I still misjudge others. I still fall short of His plan for me. I put some people up on pedestals, and I put others down. This is not right, all people are equal in Gods eyes, and I prayed to God to help me with me.

Facing one's own fears can be the toughest of all things to conquer. Waking up each morning to humiliation and guilt is difficult. It could be defeating. Shattered self-esteem and lost pride shadows every step of the day. I am no longer mad at my wife, God, or Bishop Eugene, but I am still haunted by inner doubts and nagging fears.　　　　I pray every morning for the Lord to deliver me through another day. I trust that in it He will build a better man. He will not only heal my pain, but also He will give me greater strength through it. The closer we draw to God, the greater the attack by the devil. The devil does not want us to be God's men and women. If we are to be rich in wisdom and truth, we must encounter trouble in order to apply God's truth and learn to rely on Him. It is our want and need to come to Him. This is what God wanted before the foundation of the world.

When doubt comes in we must trust the Word of God beyond our doubt. When the fear of insecurity and low self-esteem comes in, we must know and speak what the Word of God says about us! "We are more than conquerors through Him who loved us," (Romans 8:37) and "greater is He that is in us than he that is in the world." (1 John 4:4)

God's love is a very powerful tool in our lives. In the flesh, we only see ourselves. We compare our insides with the outside of others. We will never measure up. God knows when we are ready for something. He wouldn't bear weight on us that we are not prepared to carry. It would not be His design to crush us under an unbearable burden. All that comes to us He has already provided the support we need. It is ours only for the asking.

Working and paying bills is a cycle that could be discouraging. I don't feel I deserve anything. When I look at my work from a worldly perspective, I want more. My need for control and desire to have enough stuff to quell my fear stands between me and the man God wants me to be.

We all seek the approval of others until it is difficult for us to see God. The distractions are formidable. It is not all the devil's work. We do it to ourselves. He let the devil lead us astray. We know in our hearts that we should not let it happen, but we just had to know. Paul wrote, "Be of sober spirit, be on the alert." (1 Peter 5:8) Your adversary, the devil, prowls about like a roaring lion, seeking someone to devour. But resist him; stay firm in your faith, knowing that the same experiences of suffering are being accomplished by your brethren who are in the world.

"And after you have suffered for a little while, the God of all grace, who called you to His eternal glory in Christ, will Himself perfect, confirm, strengthen, and establish you." (1 Peter 5:10) Paul begins this exhortation with caution and watchfulness. We must be prepared in order not to fall into sin. We must wait on God. So many times, we charge right in and then ask God to come along. We are running out with good intentions to fix things or make things happen when we haven't been sent by God. Then we ask Him to bless our mess. He has so much more for us if we just learn to listen and wait.

We need not evaluate our situation too much. We don't need to determine if it is good or bad. Whatever the circumstance, God will use it to His purpose and to the good of His children. God gives us manna for this day, not the next. God will equip us with what we need for each day's challenge. He promises not to put on us more than we can bear. This knowledge helped me tremendously when I found myself struggling the most. God's Word is true, if only I could hang on to it. God's Word helped me to trust Him for the next day and the next challenge. Our victory and defeat is determined by our trust in God. You must choose God.

The failure to make a conscious choice is still making a choice by default. Double-mindedness is not of God. We must make the conscious choices for whom we will serve each day. If we don't, we waiver and hear only what is pleasing to our itchy ears and comfortable to our flesh and run the risk of making the easy choice. "And if it is disagreeable in your sight to serve the Lord, choose for yourselves today whom you will serve; whether the gods which your fathers served which were beyond the Sea, or the Gods of the Amorites in whose land you are living; but as for me and my house, we will serve the Lord." (Joshua 24:15)

It is not about who is right. It is about what is right. For me, my wounded pride rather than the fact of the affair has been the greater issue. I can hide behind the affair. I can lick the wounds of my pride; but, if I just come clean with my weakness, I can get help from God. Imagine how long it would have taken to deal with my pride had it not been so mortally wounded. God is shaping me to be the man He wants in His service. Praise is to Him.

Most of our problems stem from something completely different from what we are blaming. God is the beginning and the end—every problem we have is a problem with God. Therefore, we must start with His truth in all things. It takes honest self-evaluation and soul searching to hear and receive the truth versus what is in the way of it. It's very hard to admit because what you see can be bad and a rebound to the real problem. Once the real problem is exposed and revealed, the previous need is not nearly as significant.

Pride is something that God hates, and I was full of it. It still gets in the way today. I have to constantly keep my flesh under subjection because it wants to have its own way. I am often tempted to focus on the flaws and imperfections of others. I want to deflect the blame from me to them. My flesh cannot admit fault; it does not seek forgiveness. It desires control and has no concern for others.

How could this possibly be worse than adultery? I'm not living in denial, but the perception is still there. A person who makes mistakes but loves God will seek His will, and God will make his paths straight. But someone who does not sense his need for God will struggle in his own way, never finding understanding or true peace. "God opposes the proud but gives grace to the humble." (James 4:6)

Much like what is going on in most churches, we point the finger at folks with needs and highly esteem those who look like they have it all together. But nothing is what is seems; people are the same on the inside—frail, flawed, fallen. The difference is that those who have been forgiven should live a life of gratitude with compassion for those who don't see their sin rightly. And none of us are immune to sin, but praise be to God for "though he stumble, he will not fall, for the Lord upholds him with His hand." (Psalm 37:24)

I COULD PROBABLY WRITE ANOTHER WHOLE BOOK ON SOME OF THE SERMONS AND LESSONS THAT I HAVE LEARNED FROM BISHOP T.D. JAKES. GOD HAS A PLAN FOR ALL OF OUR LIVES. NO MATTER IF WE WERE HAGAR'S BABY, (BORN ILLEGITIMATELY), OR WEATHER YOU HAD A DREAM LIKE JOSEPH TO BE THE FUTURE RULER OF ALL ISRAEL.

IN HIS BOOK ENTITED HE- MOTION. HE TALKS ABOUT STRUGGLES THAT MEN HAVE THAT THEY WOULD NEVER DEAL WITH OPENLY. HE ALSO PREACHED A THREE PART SE-RIES ENTITLED " FOR EVER A VICTUM, I DON'T THINK SO". JUST BECAUSE I'VE EXPERIENCED SOME TROUBLE DON'T MEAN I HAVE TO STAY IN IT! HE WHOM THE SON HAS SET FREE IS FREE INDEED.

Chapter 10
"Know God, Know God.
No God, No God? I Didn't Know."

THE GREAT LOVE I HAVE FOR THE CHURCH AND MY THOUGHTS ON TRADITION AND RELIGION

When we were young, my older sister, in the church, Patricia, told us if we didn't receive the Holy Spirit before the clock struck midnight and Jesus came, we would be lost and go to hell. So I really wanted to get saved. The interpretation was off a bit, but the message of getting to know Jesus was clear. I owe my very life to the establishment of God's Church, even though the church is flawed. The Church has done things that are not biblical, but it has still provided me with guidelines. Those guidelines have helped stabilize me as a person. At an early age, I found security through rules and guidelines that was critical to my growth in the Church. Even when my parents were removed from the Church, they still made sure we went to Sunday School. The Lord provided us with adults in the Church who kept us in line and taught us the Word of God. As children, we were excited about God. We were young and innocent and wanted to be in His presence. The prayer and tarry services were held on Monday nights. At this service, we sought the Pentecostal experience. I believe that we did things that weren't necessarily biblical due to a lack of knowledge, but all of my early experiences have had a positive effect on my life. God uses all things for the good of those who love Him (Romans 8:28).

I initially sought the Holy Ghost out of the fear of missing the boat. I believed I would go to hell. Although this was an infantile approach to God, it was, nevertheless, a fruitful one. Because I always wanted to be in church, I was bound to know more about God. Even then, God was preparing me for the days ahead. He was preparing me for the day I would suffer at the hands of a man of God--a person I respected and with whom I served the Lord. God impressed upon my heart and mind the awesome power He has in our lives to sustain and to transform our beings from flightless creatures to soaring eagles. It was with this knowledge and assurance that He led me into the revelation of the affair between my wife and Bishop Eugene.

Our church had services just about every night of the week. Weeknight services involved the congregation. Tuesday nights was "Willing Workers Service," which was led by ministers who needed practice preaching. A bible class service was held on Wednesday nights that was led by the pastor. Thursday was choir rehearsal. Friday's service was the young people's service which was led entirely by the youth of the church. Saturday's usually centered on visiting another church out of town or attending a monthly state council meeting, and on Sundays, we had two services.

I was there for a lot of these services. When I finally received the Holy Ghost, I was pumped to do God's work. I would take my bible to school. I didn't mind telling people about Jesus.

I became really self-righteous because I didn't have balance in my life. I was deeply enmeshed in the church and the activities which gave me a sense of superiority. I thought I could be good and be above it all. Finding the right balance in life without overdoing it is a challenge for most people. Thankfully, if we don't find that balance, God pushes us into it. The Church is not perfect. We are not perfect. We cannot attain perfection through the Church; however, God works through this imperfection to bring us to Him. This is His design. Some say they won't force religion on their children. They say they will let their children decide for themselves when they are older. If we were to take this approach with food and nutrition, our children would probably die at an early age. Where would I be if I had not heard the Word and received the Holy Ghost if I had not been in church? Yes, the Church is imperfect, but God is perfect. It was in His house where He called me and filled my heart with His spirit.

The dilemma that I faced was between tradition and religion. I always felt like there were more people going to Heaven other than Pentecostals, or folks that spoke in tongues. I couldn't get it in my spirit that by simply wearing pants (if you were a woman) you would ensure your going to hell. I was taught that all of us were sinners saved by God's grace, which is true, but this is only part of the truth.

For me, understanding that I was the righteousness of God changed my life. What frees me up and holds me responsible all at the same time is the blood of Jesus Christ, which was shed for us to make us right and in right standing. When I sin or make mistakes, all I have to do is confess it, and Jesus Christ says that He will release me from all unrighteousness (1 John 1:9). We don't have a reason to feel guilty when Christ died to set us free from sin and condemnation.

Both I and my wife were trapped by the very condemnation from which Jesus Christ died to set us free. Paul said, in Romans 8:1, "There is therefore, now no condemnation to those that are in Christ Jesus." This means that if we sin, we simply confess our sin, and we are free not to have to walk in the condemnation of it. The very first time that my wife slept with the Bishop, she should have been exposed to confession and forgiveness. Instead, the Church, religion, and tradition forced her into a corner of fear, guilt, and unimportance. Also, the truth is, if we continue in this pattern, or lifestyle, we start to see it as normal or correct. We tend to want to embrace it and enjoy it. We look around and see the pleasures of sin and the fact that others are doing it, and that comforts us. It's called sin for a reason—it's a dangerous trap set up to imprison God's people—all in the name of being more like Jesus.

The danger is jeopardizing our relationship and inherited right to the kingdom of God over religion, and tradition. I've discovered that religion can come in a number of different forms. It's not just being self-righteousness, or justifying one's corrupt behavior. Religion has to do with loving anything more than you love God. (and you know what I mean). Just because they did it back then don't mean that it was right.

Tradition teaches us the facts, but facts change when new data is presented.

Chapter 11
"A Marriage Made In Heaven."

THE REMNANT – A TROUBLED MARRIAGE

Marriages may be made in Heaven, but we have to live them out here on Earth. Perhaps the Heaven part is the courtship and engagement, and reality steps in with the, "I do." Living together everyday washes away the exterior glaze of premarital bliss. The familiarity of everyday living also begins to erode the difference given to the one we love. Quite possibly, the things I did to get my wife were not the things I was willing to do to keep her. Prior to marriage, I made her the center of my attention. I looked deeply into her eyes. I tried to keep it exciting, and for me the chase factor kept the relationship fresh. Once my wife said, "I do," I relaxed. I became casual and less aggressive in the overall excitement of our new lives together. I took more things for granted. I was complacent, but I still loved her. Marriage can sure make you feel bogged down with all the concerns and frustrations that come along with it. I loved her, and she was special to me. But with all of the hustle, I lost something. In the beginning of the marriage, my wife wanted what I wanted. I had laid out certain desires and goals before we married, and she agreed to them.

Honest communication was the real problem in our marriage. I had all my thoughts and concerns about marriage, but I failed to know fully what her concerns were. We both had strong biblical values, so if there was a disagreement, we used the Bible to give us the final decision.

The devil divides and conquers. He had us to ourselves enough until he was able to cause us to justify our behaviors and actions. Everything was a cover-up for everything else. This is where our lives became a lie. You can get so far out there until you can't get back, and my wife got caught in an undercurrent. This is when we give others the right to choose for us. And consequently, this affected my marriage and threatened our future as a couple and a family.

God had shown me homosexual behavior in one of the sisters at our church, who was involved with my wife. I honestly believe if we didn't move to Memphis, she would have destroyed our family. Without you even knowing it, the devil can and will come in and take over everything you have, save for the mercy and grace of God. Our marriage was a mess. The frustration was almost unbearable. All I ever wanted to do was be a good husband and father to my kids, but then I found myself ending up with a recipe for disaster. My pain was great, and I think that her pain was worse because she had become numb.

Both of us were in bad shape. My wife began to disregard certain desires and goals that we made prior to marriage. Just as I began to slack off and disregard her and her desires, distance grew between us. The woman I loved and lived with wanted something different, regardless of what we had agreed on. Her attitude loudly told me that she would do things her way.

I sought counsel in the Church, but it wasn't the practical counseling I needed. The Church didn't address the basics such as managing finances, raising kids, managing time, continuing education, setting goals, and assessing results. All of these things are a part of life and are a concern to God. When these issues are left unaddressed, we are ill-equipped for the day-to-day rigors of life. And so, my wife and I went into marriage, the union of two souls with two vastly different backgrounds, without a clue. Both of our parents were excited for us, but I wish someone would have stopped us. I wish someone would have told us the truth about our situation. I wish someone would have stopped me in my tracks and asked me, "What in the hell do you think you're doing?" I still think I would have married my wife, but I don't think I would have married her at the time I did.

To win Cookie as my wife, I gave it my all. She was who I wanted at the time, but not necessarily who I needed at the time. She was pretty, talented, and smart. We had a strong attraction for each other. She could start a sentence, and I could finish it. We clicked. She was saved and had grown up in the Church--how much could go wrong? What I really needed was to get my relationship with God stronger, to mature, and to get my hormones in check. Hindsight . . . .

How much could go wrong? Didn't the devil say this to Eve at the tree of knowledge of good and evil? Such a perspective is a gross and heinous deception. Rather than such an insouciant approach to the decisions before we make them and He has provided an advocate to see us through. Even in the aftermath of poor decisions, He will speak to us and use them to further our growth and minister to others through them.

As young people, we often feel as though we don't have options. In matters of love, we either get married or live in sin. As Christians, it is difficult to make the latter choice. This is by God's design. We must remember this. God is greater than a little trouble. As a matter of fact, He said He would be to us a very present help in trouble (Psalms 46:1). By God breathing life into us and making us living creatures, He provides for us our escape—only a breath away. He says in His Word that He would make a way of escape for us. So why are we worrying about what God has already worked out? Church leaders should give us the Word of God and leave judgment to God. Then we would be free to handle our difficulties. Trust in the Lord is contrary to judgment. To hear and follow God's Word will help us when our minds can't handle the strains amid difficulties of our flesh. We have to be transformed mentally which is where the battle rages. The peace of God is revealed to us when we look to Him in the mirror dimly and trust Him. Our faith in God is essential here.

God speaks to us in our most difficult and critical situations. This is where He is in the trenches of our experiences. His desires are to reveal His power within the impossible. It is He who will heal our hurts and reveal His glory. I have found that through my troubled marriage, God has given me opportunities to glorify Him. What opportunities? How? My hope is in God. There is so much that God wants to do through us and in our experiences. There are so many souls that will hear God's Word through our testimonies. The devil attacks the family like no other single entity. The Church is the bride of Christ. It is in this union that He loves and nurtures us. The marriage of a man and woman is no less. In marriage, we become one, just as the Church became one with Jesus Christ.

It is our marriage that God chooses to hone and sharpen in service to and edification of Him. The closer we draw to God, the greater the devil works to separate us from Him. The greatest struggles are not the dope dealer or the prostitutes. Satan attacks our Holy oneness in matrimony and our one on one relationship with the Father. God must come first in our lives, above all other things (Matt. 6:33). God so loved us that He gave His only Son for us so that we will be forever together with Him for eternity.

If our union with God is strong and our relationship with Him becomes our priority, we will eliminate access for the devil to get in. Satan uses dishonesty and fear to create havoc in our relationships, and then he watches dishonest, insincere people destroy themselves. The same is true when there is division in the marriage.

My marriage had been troubled from the beginning because the devil saw our potential from the start and purposed to end it. I thank God that He has given us the opportunity to come together and to bring Him glory by working through our struggles and honoring Him. Tribulation humbles us, so that God can use us to serve Him out of our humility. In this, we are enriched with the knowledge that it is He who enables us and not us who enable Him. Ezra 9:8 says, "And now for a little moment of grace has been shown from the Lord, our God, to leave us a remnant to escape, and to give us a nail in His holy place, that our God may lighten our eyes, and gives us a little reviving in our bondage."

It's the suffering with Christ Jesus that allows us to reign with Him in glory. There is a deeper appreciation and gratitude that comes from what was not understood to something that was made clear. Now I can see what was always there, but I could never see. On some level, it was hard not to see, and on another level, it was impossible to know! It was a trouble that I could live with and a trouble that I couldn't live without. It made no sense to me, and it made complete and total sense to me all at the same time.

Just as He did with His remnant in Israel, He will further His kingdom with the remnant of our marriage. I have learned so much about how to be a better husband and how much Jesus Christ loved me through this experience. I have often been extremely wrong and outside of God's will and plan for my life, but He never stopped loving me. Often times, we don't evaluate things well. We find ourselves far from good judgment, but to love and forgive each other is always the right answer. God knows everything, and He was before, during, and beyond all other situations.

By thinking I was responsible for my life, I found myself drifting away from God's purpose. The professional tennis tour was my life. Tennis was like a god to me. Without things working out the way they did, I might never have seen the error of my ways. Where one has needed to be forgiven, in a great way, there was created a great love, and the ability to forgive others. All of a sudden, other's sins are not as great to you, because you can see the ugliness of your own.

God is dealing with me. He is forcing me to see the end of me and where He truly begins. The real me is not pretty, but God's grace is abundant! How much He really loves me is breaking me, and I am grateful to God for that.

I WAS LOST FROM THE VERY BEGINNING. I WAS TAUGHT THAT "THE MAN" WAS IN CHARGE, AND THAT WAS MY DOMINATE WAY OF THINKING. IT WAS THE WAY THAT I

WAS TAUGHT AND THAT WAS ALL THEY KNEW. GOD CRE-
ATED MALE AND FEMALE TO RULE AND HAVE DOMINION
TOGETHER. GENESIS 1:26-28. GOD ALSO SAID THAT WE WERE
TO SUBJECT OURSELVES TO EACH OTHER. EPHESIANS 5:21.
OUR WIVES HAVE INFLUENTIAL AUTHORITY, AND WE, AS
HUSBANDS HAVE POSITIONAL AUTHORITY. BOTH CAN BE
ABUSED. IF WE DON'T UNDERSTAND THE PURPOSE OF A
THING ABUSE IS INEVITABLE.

Chapter 12
"No Pain, No Gain."

PATIENCE AND A THRESHOLD FOR PAIN

We need patience and a substantial threshold for pain to make our way through difficult challenges in our lives. The catch-22 is that we acquire patience and a threshold for pain through these challenges. As a tennis player, I didn't walk out onto the court for the first time with the skill I presently have. It took instruction, discipline, practice, competition, victory, and defeat to build me into the player I am today. Why do we expect to meet life's challenges as fully-equipped humans? It is through our life experience that we become equipped. We shouldn't get too excited about anything good or bad. There is such a thin line between what we see and what we don't. The extremes in our lives, such as riding high or lying low, cause us to miss the real anointing within the moment. If we focus too much on good or bad, we tend to lose something powerful in the process. We close the door for the Holy Spirit to reveal the truth beyond our understanding of the moment. We shut the door on the next step God has laid out for our lives. Our evaluations invite the planting of seeds of doubt by Satan, and we lose sight of God's purpose for our lives.

It is completely fine to ask any questions we have of God, but we need to be sure our intentions are to be "like" God and not to "be" God. Whatever befalls us, whatever our questions, we must trust that it is by His will that we are where we are. Christ prayed in the Garden of Gethsemane, ". . . Father, if Thou be willing, remove this cup from me; nevertheless, not my will, but Thy will be done." (Luke 22:42)

Sarah and Abraham were given a promise from God that they would have a child in their old age, and not only that, but Abraham's descendants would be as many as the number of stars in heaven. This was an opportunity for the development of patience and trust. Sarah, in her impatience, gave Hagar to her husband to be his lover. Ishmael was born to Hagar and Abraham, and a new pain was born to Sarah. As a result of their disobedience, Sarah and Abraham grew inpatient in their trust of the Lord. They saw that their pain was bearable and hoped that it would someday be replaced with joy. And it was. Even after the birth of Isaac, God told Abraham to sacrifice Him (more pain, but God was developing and maturing Abraham through His experience).

Had God just given Sarah and Abraham a child without taking them into the wilderness, it would not have brought them closer. Their descendants would not have been given the rich heritage of the covenant between God and Abraham. What great blessing was given to all of us through Abraham, Sarah and even Hagar!

There is a master purpose behind everything that God does. He makes no mistakes, and He does all things well. In our pain, God gets rid of all the impurities. He also equips us for the challenges that we will have to handle in the future. To walk in God by faith, we must first learn to crawl. If Ishmael had been the answer to God's promise, Sarah would have lived life knowing that it was she who made it happen. Instead, God made her wait past the point of reason, and then He gave her a son. There was no doubt that Isaac was a gift from the Lord. It was so much so that Sarah laughed in response at the thought that she would conceive a child. It was ludicrous.

It is through our ability to endure pain and to grow through it that we become better servants of God. It is what defines a true child of God. Ours is to please God. God told me that if I would be faithful, He would deliver me. The despair I felt when my wife told me she was basically a whore for Bishop Eugene is impossible to convey.

I cannot comprehend how she was able to live with herself knowing this was not the way she was raised. She was an intelligent woman who could have been anything she wanted to be. She chose to be someone she despised. I watched her decline. Sin ate at her as if it was cancer. Her nails were brittle and worn. Her hair stopped growing, and her once naturally voluptuous breasts had become noticeably small. I thought having children had diminished her womanly shape, but her physical decline was the consequence of the punishing sin she held so tightly. Her life was a mess, which meant our life was a mess. She was worried about the revelation of her sin and the embarrassment of her flawed humanity. She knew better, yet she chose worse. I was afraid in our home. It was an evil presence, and I struggled with it not knowing what it was all about. It was like the house wanted to swallow me up. It was like the walls had a heartbeat of its own.

God is always looking for soldiers who aren't afraid of losing their life for His glory. Our trials and tribulations aren't about us. God is doing a greater work in our lives for the benefit of others. I have no doubt that my wife and I will make it as a couple, but we still experience the same struggles as everyone else.

Because of the journey we have already taken on a rough road, we have gained so much more. My seemingly devastating wounds forced me to see God's incredible love for me, which I realized renders all burdens impotent. The corruption in our relationship has been replaced with the presence of Christ in our lives and in our home. He is the advocate who fights the battles for us.

The first time we attempt something new, we are naturally cautious and uncertain of what the outcome will be. With no reference point, the initial experience is alarming. If extended, the experience can be overwhelming. However, the second experience is less fearsome. We learn to face what is at hand. If we don't experience pain, we don't experience joy. Life is flat, and we are simply moving through it. It is the difference between just playing church and honorably serving the Lord.

There are times when my wife can be so bull-headed, but this is how she has made it without losing her mind. As in the past, there will be times when I won't want to go on, because I am too proud. But I will remember God's love for me and the peace He has given me in the past.

Just when I thought peace would never again grace my life, I will remember how He has not treated me the way I deserve to be treated. It is because of our experience and pain that we are becoming the expressed image of God. My wife's pain and hurt helps me to struggle past my own pain and to see through the mask of the woman to whom she is, rather than the woman she looks like, or what she did.

I played the piano and sang a song I wrote for our wedding entitled, "God Made Me for You." If I knew that then, why would I want to question our marriage now? It would be convenient to say that we have grown apart, but the reality is that God didn't make a mistake in putting us together. This is His will for our lives, and with it He will fulfill His promises and His plan. We must wait patiently on the Lord and be assured that He has given us His Word. His Word will not come back void.

We will only know some things in part. All the questions that come to mind and unresolved concerns are in God's hands. I probably won't ever know the true reason for what lies deep down inside of me. These are questions to which I can never ask or know the answers.

I've heard it said that the oceans are as deep as the mountains are high. Balance can be a scary thing. We don't always understand why, but the results of struggle and perseverance can be amazing.

I still would like to know what it was that kept the relationship going between my wife and Bishop Eugene. This would only stir up more frustrations, but I can't help but wonder about their showers together and their midnight adventures--those times they joked at my expense, portrayed me as one who didn't take care of his woman. I'm the one who allowed the door to open to other men. All of these thoughts and images are a tough pill to swallow.

It is also interesting that I am actually the age that Bishop Eugene was when he started being sexually involved with my wife. He was around 46 or 47 years old. At this age, I can do much more with my mind and my body than I could do at 25 or 26.

I am much more mature and much more patient. I am probably more sexually active. I could go for longer periods of time than I could when I was younger. I know my body better. I understand the female body better. At my age now, younger women are appealing. Younger women can excite older men sexually. I understand that it is not all speed, but rhythm, timing, and speed. I guess I can't blame Bishop Eugene in those thoughts. Be it not for the mercy and grace of God where would I be? The desire to flirt is always out there. It makes my blood boil to imagine what it was like for them. The weakness of my flesh and the availability to sin is constantly before me.

With an older man and a younger woman there is power, sex, lies, and corruption. All of this was happening in the church, the one place that I thought I could go to for protection from pain and hardship. Regardless of the relationship you have with people, some things should be off limits. The basic respect that people should have for others should amount to something. If I am your friend, you shouldn't let me drive drunk. You shouldn't let me lose my life for a pleasurable moment. Bishop Eugene was much more than that to me. He was like a father. He was my hero in the sense that he loved God and had the respect of so many.

I can remember when my wife and I were having problems. I didn't know what was going on or what to do. This was during the time of the affair. I suggested over and over that we go to Bishop Eugene for counseling. My wife refused, except one time. Can you imagine being in a counseling session with your wife and her lover? I had no idea that this would be possible. What a fool I was. In some strange way, I think my wife was trying to help our marriage. Where else were we supposed to go? What else could I have done? She was miserable, and so was our family.

Bishop Eugene tried to give us counsel, but his suggestions didn't make sense to me. I walked away from the counseling sessions with nothing useful. He might have been supporting his own cause and justifying his behavior. In the counseling sessions, Bishop Eugene would use general terms like "needing to spend more time together," or "going out to dinner." These were all good suggestions, but not practical. Not every couple desires to do this, especially with limited resources and time. However, I was desperate and willing to do whatever it took. My wife was disconnected, and our life was falling apart.

WE WEVE CLEARLY IN TROUBLE, BUT GOD WAS AS CLOSE TO US AS THE AIR THAT WE WERE BREATHING. PSALMS 46.1 WHEN YOU ARE HURTING IT'S HARD TO REALIZE THAT YOUR PAIN WON'T ALWAYS BE THERE. IT'S A TEMPORARY OVER AN ETERNAL SITUATION. I WOULD RATHER IT BE BAD FOR A MINUTE WITH GOD, OR ETERNALLY, THAN IT BE RIGHT WITH MY STRUGGLE FOR A MINUTE WITHOUT GOD. I'VE GOT THE PROOF THE HE HAS NEVER LET ME DOWN, EVEN IN MY PAIN GOD IS STILL THE MOST STABLE, AND CONSISTENT THING ABOUT MY LIFE.

Chapter 13
"I Don't Want To Be A Role Model."

MY ROLE AS A FATHER

As a father, I feel responsible for my family. My wife and I are responsible to train our children in the way they should go. God instructs me to love and cherish my wife as Christ loved the church for which He died and rose again. This is a pretty tall order for men. After all, wives aren't exactly easy to love all the time, but then neither are husbands. Because of the affair between Bishop Eugene and my wife, my role as a father had been made more challenging. My responsibilities were the same as any father, but I carried more baggage as the father in the home. It is easier to allow the devil to sow seeds of doubt and division because of our battles from the past.

Biblically, I had the right to leave my marriage but was being led by the spirit to stay. I look to the future with hope, healing, and understanding. I must be more in touch with God concerning His will and purpose for my family. I know that I need to stay with my children and be a father to them in our home. I want to do this. At times, my pain returns. I dwell on what has happened which sends me into a deep depression. I am not the father I want to be since this happened.

With time, these feelings have occurred less frequently and with less impact. Time is a true healer. Like any illness, time, with proper treatment, will lead to full recovery. I need both to prevent an infection and provide a scab. God's love and grace are what helped me make it from day to day.

I look at my children and hope they are mine. The oldest daughter looks like me. My son has a long face like me and dark skin like me, but he looks like his mom. The reality is that it could have been a coin toss as to who is the biological father. My wife admits there was unprotected sex during the affair, so don't know for sure. If I let this become an obsession, it just tills the ground for Satan to plant his seeds of destruction. Joseph, the earthly father of Jesus, had to face similar doubts and questions. He was assured by the Lord of the impending birth of his child and that he was conceived by the Holy Spirit. But the faces of his family and peers must have been accusing. Just because God calls us to serve Him and to be a part of a miracle does not mean that our human nature will no longer nag us. God sustained Joseph in the days before and after the birth of Christ, but it couldn't have always been easy. Being a father isn't easy, but God sustains me in my role as a father.

It is in my family where God has both challenged and blessed me. What seems to be the most difficult for me are the mind games the devil plays on me. He reminds me of what happened and tries to corrupt the love I have for my wife with resentment of God for allowing this to happen. I know what happened was the will of God, but out of the blue, the devil will whisper otherwise. A thought will appear out of nowhere. Satan knows I am vulnerable, and he is experienced in our weakness.

Being a father and head of the house is not nearly as attractive as one might think. Fathering children and being a father are two different things. There are tremendous responsibilities in truly being a father. Most of the dicey issues that families don't really want to deal with fall to the father. The man of God who is given this position by God is called to nurture and protect his family, as well as to provide for them and to love his wife and children--not an easy task.

At times I would sincerely like to relinquish my family responsibilities. Setting curfews, disciplining children, setting budgets, and laying down the law are thankless jobs and one for which many of us are ill-prepared.

Thankfully, we don't have to learn it all in a day, although some days it feels impossible to do. If we are honest, we all have to admit that we want our children to be good reflections of us. Their flaws and failures will point to our own. Humility is thrust upon us when a child enters our hearts and homes. Because we want our children to do right and well, we can become control freaks and find everything they do to be "a hill to die on." I constantly need God's help in picking my battles. The battles that matter are the ones between the flesh and the spirit--clearly, an ongoing battle. My personal struggles are mixed with those of my children.

Perhaps this is God's way of teaching me so that I can guide them. God is not a God of coincidence. As fathers, it is important for us to instill values and not to focus on negatives. It is much more difficult to instruct rather than correct. Complaining about a problem comes much more naturally than working to find a solution. Letting a rule slide is much less a trouble than upholding it. God is the same today as He was yesterday and as He will be tomorrow. His truth abides. We must strive to be as consistent, honest, loving, and just as our Lord is with us.

The Word of God is the foundation on which we live our lives. It is through His Word and with His help that we can bravely face fatherhood. God promises throughout Scripture that He will never leave or forsake us. Even when we mess up miserably and are clueless in raising our children, God will help us. We must continually seek His faith, His wisdom, and His resolve. There is no more humbling position than that of parent. Part of the frustration and hardship associated with being a parent is our old nature we inherited from Adam. Yes, we are born again, but we are still flawed and creatures prone to sin. We must grow through God's Word in our experiences. It is a process, and all of us are "work under construction."

As a newborn, we desperately need help for everything. Words mean nothing until our brains have properly developed, and they are able to associate tangible with intangible. The Christian walk is no different. While we are being fathers, we are still children having to find out the hard way. For some, we learn the really hard way. As a result we often feel hypocritical and weak as parents. We are accountable to God just as our children are accountable to us.

Mistakes are a part of life and a vital part of our development. It is how we handle mistakes and evaluate them that make the difference in how we develop. Everyone needs space for repentance and reconciliation in order to effectively recover and move forward. Only God can bring the clarity needed in the midst of our muddled humanity; thankfully, He does.

The family is where Satan can get the most bang for his buck. In no other institution are there people more tightly knit. From the very beginning, God told Adam to be fruitful and multiply. He speaks of a man leaving his mother and father and cleaving to his wife. God desires for our quivers to be full, meaning that children are a blessing to a family. It makes Him happy. If we neglect or abandon our children, we have turned our back on God's plan for our lives and the gifts He has entrusted to our care. To be a father to my children as God directed, I must be there for them every day in our home.

I stated earlier that biblically, I had the right to leave my wife, but the Lord told me this was not His will for me. I don't believe He has called me to stay just so I can be with my children. No, He has called me to commit to the family He has given me and to love them as He has loved me. If my pride or hurt becomes more important than obedience to God, I have set myself up as my own idol. I must die to my flesh daily and love my wife as I do my own body (Ephesians 5:28). The reality is that my flesh will get in the way. Thoughts of the past will creep in, and I will need God to help me through it. Plus, I have struggles of my own that extend beyond the affair.

I am completely human and have desires which cause inconsistencies in my walk. It is easy to justify my behavior and to become complacent and therefore inconsistent. Children are particularly sensitive to inconsistencies in their parents. As teens, they seem to have kept a parental inconsistency log so that when called on the carpet, they can present it in their defense. So, what's new? We can wallow in self-doubt and fear of exposure or we can go to God.

The ability and strength to make up your own mind is extremely important. I am committed to my marriage and my kids. I have made up my mind, and I have told the devil that. He has launched a strong, aggressive attack against my decision, but because I have made up my mind, it's harder for him to stop God's will for our family. It remains a struggle at times, but because we have not reserved a way out, God has blessed us to make it and grow from it.

Prayer and fasting along with the Word of God will lead us to the right decisions. Psalm 119:105 says, "Thy Word is a lamp unto my feet and a light unto my path." Who would want to lead their children down a dark path? Not I. Without the truth and the light of God, darkness will prevail.

"Then I said to you, 'Do not be terrified; do not be afraid of them.' The Lord your God, who is going before you, will fight for you, as He did for you in Egypt, before your very eyes, and in the desert. There you saw how the Lord your God carried you, as a father carries his son . . . " (Deut. 1:29-31) I am the father of three and can do no less than the Lord has done for me. The devil constantly struggles with me about what my rights are, and the warfare in my flesh is great. But greater is God and His purpose for my life and the hundreds of thousands of lives that will be blessed by our obedience to Him!

GOD, AS FATHER, WAVIED ALL HIS RIGHTS AND GAVE HIS SON FOR OUR REDEMPTION. HOW IS IT THAT I SHOULD HAVE A PROBLEM WAVING MY RIGHTS AND GIVING UP ON MY FAMILY, JUST BECAUSE OF A PROBLEM. HE WAS THE CREATOR OF EVERYTHING. ALL POWER, STRENGHT AND AUTHORITY WAS IN HIS HANDS, AND HE KNEW THAT WE WOULD REJECT HIM BEFOREHAND, AND HE DIED FOR US ANYWAY! THIS HELPED ME TO MAKE UP MY MIND ON A WHOLE LOT OF DIFFERENT LEVELS.

Chapter 14
"Insemination."

MY WIFE AND HER PAIN

When dating two men, a woman's life might be exciting at the time, but in the life of a married woman, it is not. My wife was raised in the Church. She knew what was right, but nevertheless, she found herself in a situation that was way over her head. Job 24:15 says, "The eye of the adulterer watches for dusk . . . " Dusk is probably the hardest time of day to see. It is not light enough to see clearly and not dark enough for our eyes to have adjusted. The hazy lapse between day and night is an opportune time for a thief to steal what is not his. Bishop Eugene watched for dusk and took what was not his.

Had my wife not been ripe for the picking, Bishop Eugene would have gone on to the next wounded victim. His desire was to please his flesh, and he had taken his eyes off of the author and finisher of his faith—Jesus Christ. Unaware, the crafty snake had maneuvered himself completely around Bishop Eugene and squeezed the spiritual life out of him. Now, he is totally under the spell of darkness. Bishop Eugene has no desire to change because he is sucked in like an undercurrent.

His conscience is shattered and his senses are dull and useless. He is like a hungry lion that hasn't eaten in weeks. He is willing to wait for he knows that his meal will be worth the wait. His mind is focused; his body craves, and his thoughts are intensified upon the game. He knows how to play the game well. There is no regard or regrets. There is no fear to a mind that is not scared to do evil.

I don't believe that any woman can easily give herself to two men. While the scripture tells husbands to love their wives, wives are told to submit to their husbands. We breathe naturally without anyone telling us to do so. Why then would Scripture waste words telling us to do something we already are doing? Obviously, husbands loving their wives and wives submitting to their husbands are contrary to their basic nature. I do not believe women, particularly Christian women, typically participate in sex recreationally. Hollywood would like for us to believe this, but when women make love they are giving themselves to a man. They receive him. The parallel between the physical and spiritual for women is undeniable. This openness and vulnerability so deeply involves the woman's soul that to give herself to more than one man will dichotomize her heart.

Jesus said in Matthew 12:25, "Every Kingdom divided against itself will be ruined, and every city or household divided against itself will not stand." With little understanding, I watched as my wife diminished before my very eyes.

Her duplicitous life began to ruin her physical and mental health. Her once sweet nature turned moody, and her attitude was often sour. It was troubling to me, but carcinogenic for her. She became reluctant to attend church. I was attending Morning Prayer at church six days a week. My wife didn't even want to go on Sunday. She found church to be a place of grief and remorse with her husband beside her and her lover in the pulpit. In marriage, we are to surrender our bodies to our spouse. We are to be as one. This was not so with us. She gave herself to Bishop Eugene because she had a need--a need he abused and violated. She needed direction, and it was his job and responsibility to lead her in the right direction. She wanted direction and needed security during a difficult time only to find herself willfully walking right into the den of Satan. Bishop Eugene was definitely a wolf in sheep's clothing. Satan's desire is to dress up evil inside something that looks good. Because Satan has blinded us, our defense is too weak for his attack.

Our bullheaded, self-willed, sinful nature wants its own way and pushes to get it. It seeks power, control and attention. Pride is the vanguard of our sin. Without Christ, we are doomed. The real substance of our lives is in our hearts and whatever we do affects it. Because of this progression, sin was leading us to death. The spiritual life was literally being squeezed out of my wife. It would seem to be impossible to change once a person gets to this level, but with God all things are possible.

Christ came to Earth to teach us and to die for us, but when He returned to the Father, He gave us His spirit. Without His spirit, we cannot know Him in our hearts. In the movie *The Witness*, the Amish grandfather tells his grandson who had handled a policeman's handgun, "Whatever you take into your hand, you take into your heart."

There are really only two emotions: love and fear. All of the other emotions branch off these two. When one of the two is dominant in our lives, we either have chaos or perfect peace. At some point, if not monitored properly these two emotions will cancel each other out. Perfect love casteth out fear. Where God's love abides, there is no fear. For God has not given us the spirit of fear, but of love, power, and a sound mind. But when sin is finished, it brings forth death, but in Christ, death is but the beginning of our eternity with Him.

There is a place in every believer heart that belongs only to God. Nothing and no one is allowed in that place, but Him. Not our jobs, our friends, our spouses, our possessions, our hobbies or anything else. When we allow something else to take that place trouble is close behind. A lot of the pain is because that place that only belongs to God. For me that place is the most important thing in my life.

Chapter 15
"Too Late."

WHEN YOUR FEAR IS GREATER
THAN YOUR FAITH

Perry Joshua was a minister, my friend, and neighbor. Our occupations were different, so we didn't spend much time together. The thing we did share was our love of God. Perry was passionate for God in a way that most people will never experience. I believe that his zeal was turned toward the church rather than for Jesus Christ. He measured his life according to the people and perception, rather than the grace of God. This is just one of the traps laid by Satan for those who seek the Lord. Where better to trip us up? The closer we draw to the Lord, the greater the battle waged by the devil. God calls us to a community of believers in order to minister to each other, to worship together, and to see His face. We are to counsel one another and to pray for each other. It is here that we can be encouraged and begin to measure ourselves according to how others see us.

Perry loved the Lord, loved preaching the Word, and he loved his children. How was it that a man with such a love for the Lord and his family could take his own life? We are all broken vessels in need of God's redemptive strength in order to live freely and boldly. When we rely on ourselves, we fall. If we in the church cannot be open and humble with one another, how can we minister to those in need? How will we know another's need?

Perry had a disorder or a disease to where he had white patches in his skin pigment. He was a dark skinned brother and a lot of the patches were on his face. I knew he felt a little uncomfortable around people, but he made the most of it. I loved Perry a lot as a brother in Christ. He was just a typical father, fully committed to doing the work of Christ. He wanted to know the will of God for his life just like the rest of us. Because of the way some people pretend in the church, Perry suffered just as I did. I am referring to hypocritical people, personal ties, and behaviors--the lack of truth versus what we conveniently hide or cover up.

It is very important that I point out how much Perry loved his family. One day, Perry and his wife had an argument before they were to attend a family gathering. Perry stayed home while his wife and children went on without him. It was then that he committed suicide. He must have felt hurt--all alone with nowhere to go and no one to whom he could turn.

When a man is not allowed to be a man in his household, it is extremely damaging. I believe that it was the church that kept Perry from seeking the help he so greatly needed. His pride was probably an issue as well. Perry was a very well-spoken and respected person. He was a family man, but it was obvious that he had some insecurity in his spirit. His wife was probably struggling in some areas too. In Perry's case, ministers are supposed to be the spiritual leaders. Where do they go for help without jeopardizing their standing in the church? Fear of judgment by others forces us into a pit from which there is no escape. Unless we are able to take our eyes off of ourselves and others and put them back on Jesus, we will surely shipwreck.

When we keep our eyes fixed on Jesus, it gives us clarity and a way to wait on Him to gives us direction. The truth is hard to accept and follow. Your support systems tend to leave you alone and on your own. The crowds that supported you and loved you yesterday are no longer with you when the truth shows up. God gives us the truth, but it might not always be comfortable. The truth is liberating, yet it is difficult to grasp.

People tend to equate truth with what makes them feel better about themselves. God's truth is diluted to suit our circumstances and our unyielding grip on the world. When we are hurt by others, we are capable of saying anything to get back at them. The door is open for the enemy to cultivate self-interest, which invades our hearts and souls, like a fatal disease. Fear of discovery, failure, and abandonment drive us away from God and replace the faith given by God with fear. We look fine on the outside, but inside we are dying.

It was the most selfish thing in the world for Perry to take his life. He had a wife, three children, a church, friendships that were counting on him. We all were blessed by his gifts and talents. When your heart becomes like the sunshine beaming through a microscope, it will consume the object or the others every time. He had no chance. He was too far over the edge, lost in tradition, and starving for real love. I know he felt inadequate.

To get caught up in what looks like God and not hunger and thirst for the true and living God can be disastrous. I'm not one to judge another man's fate; I just don't know how much he loved God and how trapped in his situation he was at the time. It's like being out of jail but still being in a prison of your own making—your mind! It's hard to have to live up to the expectations of others and not be honest to the truth about yourself.

We all have struggles with people, perceptions, and what I call "the little man's complex." At that point, we have to go back to God and His Word and find out who we really are in Him. The facts are true; we are weak and make mistakes, but the Word of God says that He died for all our weaknesses. God also said that He knew us before we were created in our mothers' womb. We don't have to live our lives in condemnation and fear.

The Church has taught us not to ask questions. We blindly accept what is taught as the Word of God. Getting along and honoring the hierarchical constructs of the Church can be held above honoring God and his commands to the Church. It is easy to become a part of the system. It is comfortable because the code of conduct is quantifiable; however, it is a lie of the most egregious kind. It is like saying "clean up your act and get with the program before you fellowship with us." The traditional church expects you to get it together before you can join, or if you have joined without cleaning up, don't tell anyone. You don't clean up to take a bath. Christ meets us where we are, and loves us to Him. It becomes the Church versus Jesus Christ when they are supposed to be one in the same.

Just as Perry loved God, I love the Lord and seriously want to do what is right according to His purpose. When God changed my life and filled me with His Holy Spirit, I was excited to tell others about Jesus Christ.

Unfortunately, I went about sharing the gospel of religion more than of the love of God. I don't believe that it was intentional. I believe it was something that was handed down by people who didn't know any differently. I honestly strived to do what was right. Ignorantly, I was led to believe certain things in the Bible that weren't Scriptural, all in the name of the Church and winning souls to Christ. I was more lost than the people I was trying to lead to Christ because I was lost and didn't know it. I believe I still would have been saved and gone to Heaven, but I would have missed out on so much of God. So much of what our churches hold as dear and sacred is human fabrication handed down from generation to generation. What a gross deception It is no wonder Perry did what he did. You can go so far on the wrong side of things until you can't get back. You lose hope and you feel that you don't have any options. What we know is what makes us comfortable.

The truth is Perry took his own life. What a waste. He cheated his family and friends because he couldn't face his imperfections. Yes, what a waste. But then, any one of us could fall into the same satanic web. When my seemingly tidy life was shattered, I didn't know how I would face people (particularly those in the church who would know of the cuckolding of Glenn Williams). Fear of it happening again or losing my children would grip me until I thought it would drive me crazy. But for the grace of God, there I go. I didn't want to live, but there was something inside me that could not deny God's love for me. I believe that this was my salvation and my saving grace from the Lord, but at the time my thoughts were long from this.

A strange thing happens when we are hurting. Instead of us trying to get closer to God for help and understanding, the tendency is to draw away from Him and try to reason it out. Imagine trying to reason out the mind of God.

That is an empty thought because we can't begin to go there with Him. In our lives, there should be only trusting, believing, and receiving what God has prepared specifically for us. Our minds are not complex enough to know what begins for God, let alone the possibility of where He ends. His ways are higher than ours. He wants us to have abundant life in Him; more than what we can imagine (Ephesians 3:20). 1 Timothy 1:7 says, "For God has not given us the spirit of fear but of love and of power and of a sound mind." Doubt and confusion are marrow of the devil. He is the author of half-truths. He is an imitator and a counterfeit! He will mislead God's people and play on their good intentions while sowing seeds of doubt and misapprehension. In times of trouble, we must claim God's promise that He will never leave us and that He will give us a spirit of love, power, and sound mind. He tells us in Proverbs not to lean on our own understanding—He knows so much more! God has gone long before us. He promises to prepare a table before us in the presence of our enemies. The enemy is there, but greater is the power of Christ in our lives.

Perry's struggles were no different than our struggles. It's a betrayal not to tell the truth because of fear or losing one's self-confidence. Just because we have been given the authority to lead a group of people, we are not excused from the rule of that authority. Innocent people are suffering every day from the acts of the irresponsible minority. I personally believe that a whole country went to war, and it's affecting the entire world, because of a government of minority.

Our churches, in the 1900's, were places established to spread the Gospel of Jesus Christ and to help, protect, and care for the needs of people. They were pro-family, for hard work, and for loving your fellow believer. Children were taught to obey their parents, teachers, adults, and authority figures, but then something happened.

When the governing minority starts to lose a grip on control and experiences feelings of insecurity, you've got a serious problem on your hands. It happens, for example, in major corporations when someone, from out of nowhere, comes up with a new idea. It's also a possibility when someone has had a dream that one day blacks and whites will walk hand in hand. Maybe, it has happened to a kid that was cut from his high school basketball team as a sophomore but ended up being one of the greatest basketball players of all time.

Because I was denied the truth, I lost my way and my life, only to be given something that was beyond anything I could imagine. Only God can take what has been shattered into small pieces and turn it into new and wonderful. My prayer for Perry is that somehow God was able to give him what everybody else wrote off—what I wasn't concerned enough to find out and what others assumed was acceptable.

The church is so focused on agendas and appearances that sinners have no desire to join. I don't blame them. Perry was in so much pain. He was looking for people around him for help. The church for him was like the image of the Titanic. The help he received was superficial and limited because he couldn't truly reveal the depth of his troubles.

Perry was looking to this huge unsinkable institution, this all knowing, invincible object to fit what only God could do. A relationship with Jesus Christ and trusting Christ on an individual level is our only answer to the evil traps that are set up to destroy God's people. Hurt people need to feel comfortable about coming to God as they are not perceived, scrutinized, or judged.

You probably already sense Perry's hopelessness in this situation, but where was he supposed to go? His wife had just stripped him of his pride and the opportunity to be with his family over something that seemed incredibly small. The church had this incredible respect for him and his ministry. Because of his pride, he could not get past his pain or embarrassment. This had to be something that was going on inside of him for a while. Who could he share it with? Who would understand? His wife? His kids? His friends? People at his church, perhaps, while he was preaching a sermon? This struggle and need to be invincible is way overrated and too hard. There is only one man of invincibility, and it wasn't Christopher Reeves.

Because of the blood stained banner, I can live again. Because of the blood of Jesus, I'm set free to be honest and truthful to myself and others. I don't have to blame others or hold it against them because they don't know. People are where they are, and that's alright because we all are where we are. Nobody is mad but those who don't know and the devil.

Perry and his wife were on their second marriage. We don't like to talk about this issue as it causes more corruption and opens the door for Satan. For twenty-one days in a row, Perry and I sought the presence of God for our lives. We got up early for prayer and faithfully did that together for twenty-one days straight. It was an awesome time. I still somehow feel I let him down. Maybe I got too busy with my things and didn't take time for him.

While passing his house daily, I could have stopped one more time to tell him how much God loves us unconditionally. I should have told him that Christ meets us where we are, just as we are, and welcomes us into His arms. Holding onto religiosity spurns those who are suffering among us and betrays the commands of the Lord to love one another in humility. "If you have any encouragement from being united with Christ, if any comfort from his love, if any fellowship with the spirit, if any tenderness and compassion, then make my joy complete by being like-minded, having the same love, being one in spirit and purpose. Do nothing out of self-ish ambition or vain conceit, but in humility consider others better than yourselves. Each of you should look not only to your own interests, but also to the interests of others," (Philippians 2:1-5)

I find breaches in our contract with God at every level in this passage of Scripture. **ALL** of us are guilty, and only God can help us to become what we need to be to others and to Him. Only He can give us the mercy and grace that we need to make it. The moment we take our eyes off of Him and focus on our needs and limits, it becomes suicidal.

When I look back over my life, during this time, I as so busy doing church stuff.

I had replaced balance and reality with, rules, laws and statues. It was like serving an idol god. I was at church every morning at 6am, and on the front rows and on time for every service. It's nothing wrong with that, but I had a friend that was in trouble! Can you feel me? I feel like I lost a brother because I was so busy going to church, and doing church stuff and not being sensitive enough to the things in life that really matter to God.

(HIS PEOPLE, ALL OF HIS PEOPLE). In some ways I feel like I could have lost my family, because I was too busy doing stuff that might impress people, but mean nothing to God. It gets really stuffy, and puffy in stuff!

Chapter 16
"Growing up, and Growing Apart"

MY FRIEND, BRAD

As a youngster, my best friend was Brad Johnson. He lived right around the corner from my house, and we did everything together. Our neighborhood was a close-knit community. We lived across the street from the elementary school principal. This meant if we behaved badly at school, it didn't take long for the news to hit home. This was a great environment to be raised in. Brad was a good basketball player and one of the smartest guys I knew. He helped me get started in the game of tennis.

At the age of 14, I really committed myself to the church. Brad was into his thing and didn't necessarily want to do the church thing. Slowly but surely we grew apart. The distance between us hurt; I didn't want Brad out of my life. I kept trying to keep our friendship alive, but we were living two different lifestyles. I was in his way, and he was not interested in God. Brad quit playing tennis which eliminated our common ground. He got a job and bought a car which changed things altogether. Mobility and money enabled him to party and hang out with people who were not doing the right thing. Things seemed to come easily for Brad without too much effort. He was just one of those people.

I worked hard at mostly everything I did and especially hard at tennis. I taught myself how to play, and after two years of working and training, I earned a tennis scholarship and was able to get my B.S. in Education. After college, I played on the pro tour for four years. It was twenty years later that I saw Brad again. Somehow, the bond between childhood friends remains even when you go your separate ways. The remains of familiarity from an earlier unguarded time in our lives and a shared history bridged the years between us. Brad began to tell me how God was not there for him and how he felt let down. His mother had been really sick before she died. He couldn't understand how God could allow him to live and let her die so harshly. I listened as he talked and got it all out. He felt he was the only one who had it so tough and that God was purposely making his life miserable. He commented on my life and how I supposedly made all the right decisions and had done all the right things. My life looked easy and smooth to him. I guess he thought I was good and got better, and he was bad and got worse. Wouldn't it be nice to say I earned this?

This was my opportunity to witness to Brad about how tough times fall on everybody. Struggles are part of life, but it doesn't mean that life is against us. I began to tell my story to Brad. I watched him go from disbelief to anger, amazement, and finally to shock. He never would have believed that something like that could have happened to me. God prepared his heart to hear words that would change his life forever. That night something broke in Brad's heart.

Brad was smart, charismatic, and he had money. He was self-reliant and in control, but he could not relieve the suffering of his dying mother, nor could he find anyone else to do so. In his heart, he wanted God to spare her life. As she suffered, he grew angrier and angrier with God. Later on, Brad suffered the loss of his father and brother. As Brad listened to my story very attentively, he realized that trouble doesn't have an assigned address. It happens to all of us. He started to realize that it is how we handle our trouble that will determine our success in life.

God wants to use our mess as a message to others of His awesome power and ability in our lives. He allows us to make our own decisions. He won't make us, but He will love us, and chasten us with that love until the end.

Brad's main issues were his ways and his choices. He was always sincere and genuine. He would tell you the truth, but he would live the lie. He smoked and drank a lot, but he was not a hypocrite. This truth can be admirable in a person, but it can also turn into a cop-out that will allow you to not be responsible for your actions. You can dodge God for a lifetime with excuses and crutches, but the truth is still the truth. One day, we will have to face God for ourselves.

On the day I visited Brad, 20 years after our childhood days, he was constantly smoking and drinking alcohol. He never stopped. It was as if he was trying to cover up some pain inside or prove some kind of point. I believe it was hurt and pain, masked in booze. Brad had the ability to drink and then go to work the next day and hide it all. The same night I visited him, as I was about to leave, Brad stumbled over the coffee table and wasted everything. It was so embarrassing as he stumbled and almost fell flat on his face. I was sad. I told him that my prayers were with him and that he would always be my best friend. Sin separates, but love brings us back together. I believe Brad's life changed for the better from that night forward. It changed because love never separates. Unconditional love is not waiting for a change. I believe Brad felt this in me for the first time. We cannot change people who do not want to change. God will always be there to help us, but a person must make up his mind to change. I believe that night was Brad's start.

Brad story is a lot like Perry's. Remember I didn't even really dance with my wife until a couple of years ago. All throughout college, I would go to the dances, but I wouldn't dare dance. I remember saying to myself, all of theses people are going to hell for dancing, and shaking their booties. It was foolishness. Once again, I feel if I was a little more approachable, and accessible I could have shared more of God's love which is really what changes peoples lives.

Chapter 17
"If You Don't Know, You Don't Grow."

EXPERIENCES THAT PROMOTE FELLOWSHIP

Life can seem as though it is one long rollercoaster ride. The ups and downs can be trying as well as exciting. If we knew what to do in times of trouble, we would probably do it. However, we usually don't know what to do, so we react under stress. This whole ordeal has forced me to look at life more closely. I want to know more about God. I want to know more about my own inconsistencies. I want to avoid judging people and things I know little about. I want to help not hurt. I want to know more about how God sees things and how He deals with them.

It takes the whole of our experiences, both good and bad, to arrive at a place where we are objective enough to begin to understand the riches and depths of God's will for us on Earth. Scripture says, "His ways are past finding out." So in search of answers, I have actually stumbled into His presence. In the very center of my weakness, He has shown me His glory. This place of brokenness is one I never want to leave, for I have found peace and richness of life in knowing that He loves me just the way I am. His forgiveness and restoration is awesome and beyond compare. My carnality enjoys having fun and for everything to go well, but I will never experience the supernatural hand of God in what's ordinary.

I am crazy about the fact that God loves me, for me. To experience His touch and to have Him speak to my heart concerning issues that bother me are worth the pain. God has never failed me, and with this I trust Him with my life, knowing that His peace has no price tag. No amount of money can purchase it. It is free to all those who believe. He doesn't need us; we need Him. Because God is who He is, He could do it all himself, but He created us for fellowship with Him. We are "fearfully and wonderfully made." Christ has gone before us and has made our way. He is our shepherd and watches over us closely. We can stray and get hung up in the brush, but he finds us and brings us back into the fold. We can fight and struggle to free ourselves from the thorns that pierce our flesh and ensnare us, or we can call out for Him to help. He is right there.

I have found that the Lord is interested in the decisions of our hearts. He is not keeping a log of what we do for Him but wants us to believe and rely on Him in all things. They will know us by the fruit of our spirits and by the love that is inside us. There are many in this world who are kind and who do good deeds, but they don't know the Lord as Savior. We are fallible and will make mistakes. We have good intentions, but we fall short.

God is unlimited and sincerely interested in what concerns us. I know my wife loves me and my children love me, but there is no one who can love me like Jesus. I don't want to live this life without Him. We deny others a huge opportunity when we interfere with God's work in their lives. Struggles breed fellowship. Difficult times help us to really know God better. We appreciate each other more when we have done without or lost something that we thought we couldn't live without. When we play God by always trying to step in and prematurely pulling people out of their pain, we cripple them for life.

I wanted someone to pull me out, but I would have lost so much if they would have done it in their time and not God's time. I felt betrayed, and I thought that God had forsaken me, but all God was doing was promoting a deeper level of communion between us. What we have now is so much greater than what we had before, and I thank Him for it. How we talk now is much more meaningful. I can be honest, sincere, and up front with whatever, and I know that (as the song says) "Ain't no mountain high enough, ain't no valley low enough, ain't no river wide enough, to keep me away from Him."

Our experiences are about our maturity and our completion of God's plan for our lives. It's all about preparation. Only God knows the end from the beginnings. It's about strategy and calculated risk. Once God is able to work it all together, it's a true MASTER PIECE. ROMANS 8:28

Chapter 18
"To Serve with Love and Is God First?"

The heartbreaking affair between my wife and Bishop Eugene has shown me that there is nothing greater than God's love in our lives. The greatest thing we can offer others in their deepest and darkest time of need is God's love. The greatest healer in the lives of others is His unconditional love of them. When we reach the end of our support system in the world, God still has much more to give. God created us in His own image and gave us dominion over all things. This was done for His enjoyment because He first loved us. We fell, and He redeemed us and paid for our salvation with His blood on Calvary. Our debt was paid in full. He gave us His birthright. We are His. It is a wonderful thing to know that God's love isn't contingent on our doing what is right. If it were, all of creation would be gone. We would have destroyed ourselves long ago. Love is what regulates us and gives us objectivity when sin separates and leads us astray. We need humbling experiences in our lives to help us see the need for His love and grace. Without them, we walk around in our own glory thinking we are responsible for our good works. Humility forces us to know that apart from Him, we are nothing. Pride gives us the idea that we had something to do with it.

When we first joined the Potter's House, I wanted to establish a close relationship with Bishop Jakes because he was instrumental in the healing process of my family. The church had close to twenty thousand members, so it was impossible for me to do this. But this turned out to be an awesome thing for me. It was also good for the church body because we needed to go out and save those that were lost. God was using this experience to show me that it was Him I needed, not a man. This was the beginning of understanding for me of our commission to go out into the world to share the good news. Once you have been blessed, it is about going out and blessing others. You don't hoard information or form cliques.

We tend to attach ourselves to the ideas of the Church and can lose sight of Christ and why He came to Earth. According to Scripture, this possesses a form of godliness or self-righteousness which denies the power of Christ. We are all hypocrites to a certain extent and where better to be than in a hospital for the hypocritical. However, the church must be on guard against the stifling effects religion can have. Bishop Jakes taught us we are flawed and damaged goods in need of God's mercy and grace in our lives. For us to think that one position in the church is greater than another is destructive. It was our Lord who washed other's feet.

Jesus chose the lowest of the low to minister to. He came to save the lost. Pity and self-aggrandizement in the church is destructive. Wanting to be of value and to be "somebody" in the church is attractive and common, but the Lord mercifully brings our way in order to avert the corruption such thinking brings. The world can be more accepting and forgiving of sinners sometimes than the church. It takes one to know one.

As I worked my way through my troubled marriage, the Lord showed me that I must seek His kingdom first. Simple? Not especially. In my marriage, I probably was distracted by the demands of each day and goals I set for myself. The same holds true in the church when the institution and all of the demands of the day become the focus. God said, "Seek first the kingdom of God and all these things will be added unto you." I can't say that I love God more than anything. I still love God, but honestly, if you put it all down on paper, I love things more. My selfishness and pride controlled my life. God knew what I could handle, and He also knew that this pride issue in me had to be dealt with head on!

Our eternal life has begun here on Earth. If we keep that in mind, it sheds a whole new light on our daily walk. We are here for His purpose and to do His will. We are at the beginning of understanding God. Humbly, we must walk in His path. We must wait on the Lord. He is the way, the truth, and the light.

Chapter 19
"Today"

I sincerely love my wife and children. God gave me an incredible gift when He gave them to me. The challenges can sometimes be great. I often feel like I am on one side of the fence, and they are on the other, but life without them and the struggles would be horrible. Challenges can be scary at times, but they only bring to me a greater understanding of God and His purpose for my life. His grace is sufficient for all my days.

When I disagree with my wife, and I know she really wants me to agree, I have to go to God for affirmation in my choice. It is more important that my spirit is in agreement with God than with others. When seeking the truth, we must be prepared for the consequences. It is not always pleasant or easy. He reproves us in order to refine our character. God purges us to produce more fruit. As we grow, we can be trusted with more. After we have been proven faithful over a few things, God will make us rulers over many things (Matt. 25:23). It is not for the faint of heart. We must ask God for wisdom to choose our battles. The rewards outweigh and cannot be compared to our light afflictions along the way (Psalm 34:19).

In Texas, the expression is "pick your hill to die on." Fathers can't always be a friend to their children, nor can we always do what our wives want us to do. We are supposed to be fathers to our children and husbands to our wives first. I can't tell her everything she wants to hear, especially without God's endorsement. There is something about the woman you love that makes you weak, and only God can give a man the backbone to make the hard decisions. There are also many times when she is right when I think I am the one who has the answers. In many cases, I am wrong and God corrects me through her. God has given me the understanding not to see through her as much as to see she through. There is a difference.

Just dealing with life, minus the affair and the years of hurt and loss of trust, is a struggle. We both want what we want, and the children are in the middle not knowing what is going on. There are bills and the struggle to stay caught up. If we were ever to break up, I don't think it would be over the affair. At times, we both want different things which, looking back probably was the crux of the affair. We may want the same things but in different ways. We come from very different backgrounds, and the melding of our two experiences has not been easy, but I guess it never is for couples who stay together for life.

God is carving our struggles and our pain into something for His glory and to the benefit of others. We had made the decision to move to Memphis, TN. We felt that this would give us a fresh start. We needed to get away from that environment. It was a positive and calculated decision. My wife and children were in favor of the move, for the most part. It was a lot different than we anticipated, but the growth, rewards, and obedience to God is paying off. We have been in Memphis for about a year and a half. God has been able to break a lot of things inside of me, in order to use me for His glory.

My attitudes toward my job, self-willed, inabilities, wife, church, and my children are almost completely different now. The love and respect I have for ministry and God's work have changed tremendously, without God breaking me in some areas and crushing me in others. I know my life would have been merely lived for myself.

As God is changing me, everything changes.

I got a chance to go to Man Power in Atlanta, GA at the Georgia Dome. There, God changed my life. It was a group of the brothers from our church that chartered a bus. It was there that God showed me that my love was nowhere near what it needed to be.

I was able to pour out my heart before God and tell Him that I didn't know what to do or how to do it, and that He needed to do it, or it wouldn't be done. It has been almost a year since we went to Man Power, and I have kept my vow not to yell back at my wife.

The experience also revealed a side of me that was always hidden. I had held a grudge against my son's dog that really frustrated me. I couldn't understand why this dumb dog would run away and not come back home when we called him. We would have to spend hours chasing down the dog because once he got out of the house or the backyard, he was gone. I couldn't understand how this dog could do that, knowing that we were providing and caring for him.

At the Man Power conference, I was talking to one of the brothers about this concern, and the brother said to me, "You don't love that dog at all." It got me all upset, especially since he was struggling with cigarettes.

What did he know? How dare he say that, after all I have done for this dog, that I didn't love the dog? I paid over two hundred dollars to purchase the dog. But after I sat there and thought about it, he was right. I even had the nerve to say my son acted just like his dog. Both were ungrateful and wanted to do what they wanted to do.

I thought to myself I don't have to love the action but always love the person. Again, something broke in my spirit that would change me forever. I was finally about to see where I ended and God began. My eyes began to well with tears as it was revealed. My heart was hurting, but my life was changed for the better.

I thank God for loving us, even in our ignorance. It is with His patience with us that we are able to learn patience with others. I went back home after the conference and apologized to the dog and my son. I have a completely different outlook about people and God's love now. I hope it never changes. We all will make mistakes, but God's love is greater than anything. He can and will help us through it all.

When we are focused on ourselves, it's difficult to see what's right. When we are focused on the outside, it's impossible to know what's right on the inside. What I have learned about relationships is that they are never 50/50. You have to be willing to give and to receive, and unconditional love is the sustaining factor. I've learned that life is too short not to forgive, and we all need to be forgiven for something at times.

Only God knows everything, and we don't. Mistakes and offenses are inevitable. The greatest love is to forgive and move forward and face whatever fears we have, and then seek healing from them. Healing is surrendering to self and allowing God to prove His power in our lives. HOW DO WE SURRENDER? SURRENDER. This is a choice that we have to make every day.

We say that God is first, but in reality it's not the truth. We self serve, and operate out of our needs and wants. This is why fasting and prayer is so important. We don't even know what we need are what we want without having that presence of God in our lives to tell us what's right and what's not. By seeking God first every day, on your own, and allowing Him to have that place, gives us perspective for the whole day. Try it out for yourself for 30 days. Just 15 minutes per day. It will change your life FOR EVER!

Personal Message from the Author

What is the purpose of this book? I needed to vent my hurt and frustrations to hopefully help others. There are things I won't ever be able to communicate. This book has helped me release and heal in a number of ways. I have been able to talk to people, talk it over with myself, and talk it over with God. To be able to share with other couples and help them through my family's experience has been something extremely positive. This experience for me has been like being in a car accident. Initially, there are some aches and pains. There are possible internal injuries, possibly life-long injuries that might not be detected for a long, long time.

The "accident" has forced me to become closer to God. It has given me an appreciation for God's grace and mercy. I also was able to see how corrupt my own ideas were about being religious and self-righteous. Pride in a person is a cruel thing. It hides itself in dignity and honor, but in reality it is ugly, harsh behavior. God puts us into a certain situations for growth, maturity and revelation. Growth is birth out of revelation.

I thank God every day for this experience. It is difficult to get away from the experience because I have to see it everyday. I think this is what God is saying about His church, but His love is so great for the church that what He sees doesn't compare to His love for us. Because He knew how the story would end and because He was the creator of everything, it was easier to endure. I believe that it hurt Him, but because of the joy of having His people eternally, He endured. Jesus endured the pain because He knew that His Father loved him. He knew that He had his best interest in mind, and He knew that it would bless others. Because of Jesus' act of obedience, all of humanity was given the opportunity to receive eternal life. Our pain has helped couples all over the world reconcile. The number one job of Satan is to destroy marriages. He doesn't want to see unity, love, and harmony within the family structure and people loving, encouraging, and forgiving each other. Satan's desire is for us not to communicate with each other or to be affectionate with each other. Satan wants to pit the husband and wife against each other, causing the children to grow up failing the same way. Satan wants us to justify our behavior by pointing the finger as an excuse instead of being responsible and accountable for our own actions. With Satan, no one wants to admit to any responsibility to anything.

With God, relationships and marriages won't be perfect! Perfect is a process; perfection is a state of mind. We must understand that God makes the difference in what we lack as we do our best. He is our perfection. We will struggle at times and have differences, but committing to our relationship and our children is our responsibility. When a couple makes that commitment before God and man, right in the face of the devil, they make a deeper commitment to see that the devil fails. The devil sees unity, love, stability, and prosperity in a successful marriage. The devil sees the children who are being prosperous and the community benefiting from the family's commitment to each other. It is much easier not to commit when you are having problems. It is much easier to say we grew apart You can blame the divorce or separation on a number of things, but what about your children? What about their well-being, training, and upbringing? What type of messages are we giving to them by divorcing? How will it affect them as they grow up? Will they accept step-parents, and how will it affect them to have step-siblings? Will their new relationships be any better than your current relationship? Adultery is bad, but to destroy generations is worse. We need to seriously do our friends and family a favor and tell them the truth about marriage, just as we have about the seriousness of HIV.

We don't talk honestly enough about the truth because most people don't want to be responsible to it. As we grow and get deeper into God's Word, He will show us the truth about ourselves. He will also shed light on things that are important to us maturing spiritually. He will reveal hidden truths about life and people that make so much sense, but because we didn't know it, we couldn't see it well enough to make the adjustment.

One small example is the importance of marital vows. We repeat the words before God and man, "For better or for worse, for richer or poorer, in sickness and in health, 'til death do us part." I believe if the majority of people heard what they were saying, they would either wait to make sure, or they would not get married at all. It's so easy to get sucked into something, dishonestly. Our intention may be good, but in many cases it's lust, deception, or some type of pressure that causes us to make a life-long decision that wasn't well thought out.

The deterioration of our families is the downfall of our country. The teachings that come from home, through a stable marriage are invaluable. It is not a matter of who or what is right in many cases. It is about responsibility and commitment. God is helping others through our experiences, and He is answering our prayers at the same time. He wants for me what I have always wanted for myself. What I have been praying about all my life is what He is giving me.

There are certain desires and challenges that happen in our lives that push us into our destiny. We will often times have to pay a price to receive this anointing. God times events and challenges us right at the moment He knows that we can handle it, right at the moment of our vulnerability. God won't allow that moment to kill us, but He will allow it to take us to the very edge of our faith.

The second purpose for this book is to help couples who are struggling over issues that will be forgotten in a minute. You won't ever remember what it was if you can understand how meaningless certain issues are. There are couples who have gone through much more and are still making it.

We should think of our marital issues as a numbers game. As men, our number is on the right, and our spouse's number is on the left. The example is if the argument is not as meaningful or important to you, you score it 2 to 8. This means that you still feel that you are right, but it's not worth the energy in your relationship, over all, to fight for. Another situation might come up, and you might feel even stronger about this one than the last one, and the numbers are 5 to 9. In this scenario, it's still not enough to jeopardize the harmony of your relationship, so you decline. Now you run into a situation that is 6 to 5, meaning you know, and she knows that you are probably right, but because the numbers are not high enough overall, it's still not worth challenging her trust yet. Finally, you have a situation that you feel is life-changing for you and the well-being of your family, and the numbers are 9 to 13. Your spouse feels she's right and still won't let go because he or she usually always wins. This is the time that you should lovingly and tactfully argue. Once it's over, and everyone sees the results, the future challenges won't be nearly as difficult--by being thoughtful and considerate of others and by giving and not always taking.

The third purpose of this book is to help couples try to avoid certain innocent but potentially detrimental situations. I realize that you might think you are strong enough to handle most situations, but it still might be better to leave it alone, if there is any doubt in your mind.

If you end up in an affair with someone, it didn't start that first time you had sex. It started when you should have been investing more time in paying attention to your spouse. Instead of feeling sorry for yourself and putting your attention into someone else's opinion, you should have been seeking God for wisdom and direction--seeking God and not taking that extra peek at that other woman or man or that flirtatious smile. It is time that you can't get back and wasted feelings that could have been preserved for your spouse who desperately needs and appreciate you. To cheat on your spouse is a demoralizing experience. When trust is violated, and abuse is facilitated, nothing good comes out of it. Once a person's confidence is shattered through their trust being violated, future trust is very difficult to find. In most cases, this is something that can be avoided. It's about being honest and transparent. The problem is that if I tell you the truth, it could change your opinion of me. The truth is what makes us free—free not to allow a few minutes of pleasure destroy what it took a lifetime to accomplish.

Having an affair, or being the one who didn't have the affair, is something that stays in your spirit. Indirectly, you become that person who had the affair, because you are making love to that person who had the affair. God forgives us, but the ability for us to get over it could take a long time.

It is annoying how we are willing to give up our whole life and all that we stand for over a moment of satisfaction. You can't buy trust or loyalty that comes from a faithful and committed spouse. Things can always be replaced, but good loyal people die out and are hard to keep around. It is much easier to give up and not fight for what you know is right. The same things we don't overcome or deal with the right way in our current, rocky relationship with our spouses will turn out to be the same mistakes in your next one. It is much better to try and deal with your current wife or husband than to compound the problem by involving a girlfriend or boyfriend because they have some deep needs themselves.

It is extremely important to ask ourselves what we are really giving up when we pursue that other person. Take a good look at them. They are probably not as attractive as your spouse. They don't know you as well, so they haven't been tried like your spouse. They haven't cleaned up after you or been there through the tough times. Your wife might have had your children and helped you through school, and the list could go on and on.

Is it really worth trying to make it work? Counseling will help open up some areas that have been overlooked. If your spouse has neglected her looks or the husband is working too much, it can possibly be worked out. It is an unfair comparison to involve someone else when they can come and go and do for you and feel that this is a service to you. Your marriage is not a service; it is a commitment. It is a vow. For a lot of people, this is a big game. If they are pursuing you, chances are they are also looking at your girlfriend, too. All the while, your husband is still trying to work things out by working overtime, watching the children, cutting the yard, cooking the meals and vice versa. Too much is at stake to play a game with another person's life like that.

It is an Adam and Eve/David and Bethsheba-type of thing. Eve wanted the apple because it was forbidden. She had the garden, Adam, and was the mother to all of creation, but it wasn't enough. David wanted Bathsheba because she was not his. He had the kingdom, women of his choice, and wealth for generations, but it was not enough. We don't count up the real cost of our actions prior to making that decision out of our flesh. With Adam and Eve, sin entered the world. With David, he ended up losing his son and murdering an innocent man. We also end up unintentionally wounding our children and committing deeper sins because of our mistakes. The question is, "When is enough, enough?" It's also troubling to understand that most men want to be God and not like God.

I think it is also important to understand what temptation is all about. We need to talk about being in tough, flirtatious settings. We don't need to live our lives in denial. Married couples need to network and support each other and hold each other accountable. Monthly small marriage groups are helpful. One day, we will have to face the truth, just like one day there will be judgment. We either need to try and do it right now or suffer for it later. It is about having some oil left in our vessels. It is about knowing you did what was right, not who was right. This can be confusing to that person who's questioning and doubting their decisions.

The parable in the Bible concerning the five wise and five foolish virgins illustrates the importance of always having oil in your vessels. In the story, the virgins are awaiting the arrival of the bridegroom. The five foolish virgins get complacent and allow the oil to run out of their vessels. They go to the five wise virgins and ask to have some of their oil, but the wise virgins refused and told them to go find more of their own. While the foolish virgins are gone, the bridegroom appears. Because they were not prepared, the foolish virgins lose their inheritance. I believe that the five wise virgins had conversations with the five foolish virgins and told them about the dangers of being complacent and self-willed. So when the five foolish virgins found themselves without oil in their vessels, it was no surprise to the five wise virgins. In the same way, we all need to be accountable to someone, in terms of what is right and true. Love will always be the regulator in searching for truth and being honest and not self-righteous. If I were truly your friend, there would be no way I would knowingly allow you to go in a way that would be negative or harmful, but I would lovingly point you back to God's truth. It's important for us to daily seek God's will for our lives-- everyday, because everyday is different.

We will sin and come up short. We will need God's grace and mercy in order to make it. There is one thing that has helped me when there was nothing else that could: my need for God and His mercy, His grace and His love. The idea is not to waste what you can't get back. Our time with God is so valuable, and the time we spend together need not be wasted. To be honest, even if it's hurting, it is the first start to something secure. The issue is how we choose and what we lose in the process. You never want to lose touch with the Creator and those who really love you.

You will never know or understand either without some kind of shaking. The rest is FEAR (False Evidence Appearing Real). Our egos edge God out, but God's love puts us back in place. It doesn't matter how many times we fail; all that matters is that we get back up!!! His love won't ever leave us. But we can remove ourselves through the lust and in cognations of our flesh. Remember it is all about our choices.

Glenn

Heading in a New Direction

Moving to Memphis was one of the biggest decisions of our lives. We decided it would give us a fresh start. I personally felt the need to get out of my past environment. All of my friends and close relationships belonged to the church that caused me so much pain. I felt like a terminal disease to certain people. I dearly miss my biological family and the fellowship we had at the Potter's House, but that's about it.

I also felt there was another person who had befriended my wife. Against my wishes, she still chooses to communicate with this person. Even after all that we had gone through. I had always honored her wishes concerning people she felt that had caused threat to our relationship. I think this is a good thing for a couple, even when there might not be an attraction on the part of the other spouse to that person in question. She did not honor my request, and this was another reason for leaving. I think it is really important for us to understand that the devil hates and wants to destroy people who love and obey God's Word.

The children were confused and excited about the move. I knew this move must have been God's plan because it would affect everyone. My whole family would have to be on the same page for this to work. AND GOD WORKED IT OUT!!!

It was extremely important that we find a place to worship and be spiritually filled in Memphis. We visited a number of churches and were praying and asking God for a church that would benefit the needs of the whole family. We visited a church called New Direction. It seemed the whole church was jumping and bumping to the rhythm of the music and the rhythm of God's love and spirit. It appeared to be way too much for me and my traditional upbringing, but this was part of the reason God had to move us. God revealed to me that this ministry would challenge me and that I would start to really understand His love. I grew up learning God's judgment and fear of him, but it was absent of His real love for us. It was almost all rules and regulations. As we were trying to get a feel of what New Direction was all about, everyone we talked to had positive things to say about the ministry.

We visited the church a couple more times. Our children enjoyed the Word and the loving hip-hop atmosphere. What convinced me about the church were the preaching and the teaching of God's Word. You can feel the anointing all over the place. Apostle Dr. Stacy Spencer is the founder and senior pastor at the ripe age of 35 years old.

It is just like God to humble people. It is just like God to make people open and free to be used, so God can use them to spread His Word. When you get old and stale, you become good for nothing but serving your own purposes. The ministry, in some ways, leaves serving God and His people, and it becomes all about you. (I understand this part of being a member of the church very well.)

Pastor Stacy's love for God, his integrity and character are authentic. His willingness and his openness to the direction of the Holy Spirit is one that is at a level beyond anyone I have ever met, other than Bishop Jakes. I have known and been exposed to a lot of ministries and ministers. What most of us fail to recognize in the ministry is that the man of God is to be the man of God. His fruits are his evidence.

We are to pray for him, love and support him, and seek God so that his message might be delivered. When the man of God speaks, you want to be assured that it is God talking. This is what I hear and what I felt through this man of God. The ministry at New Direction Christian Church has turned our lives around. We have met people who have completed parts of their destiny. We started a monthly, small group couple's ministry, and it has been a tremendous blessing to us and other couples. It holds us accountable to each other.

We don't sugar-coat our experiences, and we don't have to put up a false image of the way we are supposed to be. We try to keep it real, and we talk honestly about our issues and challenges. It is much more different to be honest. It is easier to lie and cover up but walk away from the experience with nothing. Ministry should be about meeting needs and being delivered and being set free. Once we are free, we can help others with their needs and concerns.

Pastor Stacy has allowed us to continue 6:00 a.m. morning prayer on Tuesday, Thursday, and Sunday mornings. He believes in the power of prayer and the Word of God. I have learned so much about God's love, humility, and authority within the body of Christ through Him.

It was really crazy. New Direction had their annual Christmas Party, so we decided to go. It was all well organized. The food was great, and the fellowship was awesome. I had met some brother's and other couples, so we felt right at home until…

Pastor Stacy came by our table and asked if I was going to get down on the dance floor that night? I didn't want to sound overly religious, so I told him maybe so. He was such a riot that night . As the night when on we had such a great time, and guess what? I did it. I danced with my wife for the first time, and she really appreciated it. It was so much fun! And I couldn't believe it, after it was all over, I still felt like God loved me.

This was a very special moment for me, and one I will never forget! Some of our transitions were tough, but all of them fulfilled a purpose.

Without the difficulties in Texas and coming to Memphis, I would have been ill-prepared to fulfill all that God had in the future for me. God knows everything, and we receive things as He gives them to us. It is something about this scenario that we as humans don't understand. You've got knowing, but knowing is nothing until it is given by the All Knowing. We can pray these deep and spiritual prayers that are impossible to be lived without God, in His grace and mercy, don't fulfill us.

At first, the move to Memphis was a struggle. Things didn't work out the way we expected, but we always knew that it was God who brought us to Memphis. I can remember having to pull over to the side of the road and just cry. But even in the midst of my tears, I felt His undeniable presence. I heard Him tell me that I wasn't walking this one alone. He told me that I would never be prepared for my future if I didn't understand my past. We are not to stay, live, or dwell on our past, but to learn from and understand it enough to never go back to it.

The ministry at New Direction Christian Church is geared to helping broken people who are deep in their sins and WANT OUT! The ministry seeks to help people who are real and sincere about their sin but need God's love to bring them out. Good people don't understand this kind of healing that comes from the inside out, not the outside in. The ministry is about when you are desperate, thirsty, and hungry for hope, in a time of hopelessness. This is right at the point when God wants you to cry out to Him so He can help you. Many times, good people don't honestly feel a sincere and real need for God. They act like they do but really and truly don't feel they are worthy of God's goodness. Good people are good; they are inclined to justify.

Righteous people turn their noses up at people who do not look like, act like, dress like, or have the same ideas as they do. I understand this very well because I was one of them. I thought it came in how well you prayed or how well you shouted (Holy Ghost dance). It had nothing to do with any of that. God looks at your heart, and that is what New Direction is interested in.

Once again, everything God is saying to you He will back up with His Words. There is no doubt in my mind that this person would have destroyed our family. I feel that it was out of my hands and over my head. With Adam and Eve, either there would be good or evil. To stay in the Garden of Eden, they would have to obey God and surrender their will to what God's purpose was. Because they chose not to, their decision separated them from God. The same happened with us; because this person was going to remain in our lives, I felt that I had to make a serious decision, either to leave Texas, or allow the enemy to destroy, or separate us from each other. That person's influence was stronger than mine. My objectivity was weak because I was still dealing with being hurt. Being off balance leads to making bad choices.

After living in Memphis, this was confirmed. Something about Jesus Christ you have to know. We know these through faith, and allowing God to work through our experience. Faith will put you on the edge of your most horrible nightmares, but God won't allow you to be consumed. He will always, at the right time, provide a ram in the bush, just as Abraham was to sacrifice his son on an alter, and right as he had committed to do what God said, He touched him and showed him another sacrifice instead of his son. All we have to do is be willing.

God bless you, and please feel free to e-mail me, I would love to hear from you, and possibly share our experience at your retreats, couples ministry services and church, or other engagements.

1). Am I critical of others, or myself?

2). The truth is not always the truth?

3). Is it possible to be in love with some one else other than your wife?

4). Do you care if your child married into another race?

5). Can what I do be a blessing to others?

6). Is there hope beyond every failure?

7). Is it important that different races and cultures get seriously involved with each other?

If your answer is other than yes, you have been dishonestly taught and betrayed on a certain subconscious level.

We would love to fellowship with you, and to be a blessing to you. Sincerely to serve, Glenn and Earline.

Notes/Reflections

e-mail

glennwilliams_5@hotmail.com

9 781434 306326